WORDS ALONE

D0531629

Withdrawn From Stock
Dublin City Public Libraries

NO. 8 (NEW SERIES) AUGUST 1937.

A BROADSIDE

EDITORS: DOROTHY WELLESLEY, AND W. B. YEATS.
PUBLISHED MONTHLY AT THE CUALA PRESS, ONE HUNDRED
AND THIRTY THREE LOWER BAGGOT STREET, DUBLIN.

THE CURSE OF CROMWELL

You ask what I have found, and far and wide I go,
Nothing but Cromwell's house and Cromwell's murderous crew,
The lovers and the dancers are beaten into the clay,
And the tall men and the swordsmen and the horsemen where are they?
And there is an old beggar wandering in his pride,
His fathers served their fathers before Christ was crucified.

O what of that, O what of that
What is there left to say?

300 copies only.

WORDS ALONE

Yeats and his Inheritances

R. F. FOSTER

OXFORD
UNIVERSITY PRESS

OXFORD

UNIVERSITY PRESS

Great Clarendon Street, Oxford, OX2 6DP,
United Kingdom

Oxford University Press is a department of the University of Oxford.
It furthers the University's objective of excellence in research, scholarship,
and education by publishing worldwide. Oxford is a registered trade mark of
Oxford University Press in the UK and in certain other countries

© R. F. Foster 2011

The moral rights of the author have been asserted

First published 2012

All rights reserved. No part of this publication may be reproduced, stored in
a retrieval system, or transmitted, in any form or by any means, without the
prior permission in writing of Oxford University Press, or as expressly permitted
by law, by licence or under terms agreed with the appropriate reprographics
rights organization. Enquiries concerning reproduction outside the scope of the
above should be sent to the Rights Department, Oxford University Press, at the
address above

You must not circulate this work in any other form
and you must impose this same condition on any acquirer

British Library Cataloguing in Publication Data

Data available

Library of Congress Cataloging in Publication Data

Data available

ISBN 978-0-19-959216-6 (Hbk.)
ISBN 978-0-19-964165-9 (Pbk.)

Printed in Great Britain by
Clays Ltd, St Ives plc

2 4 6 8 10 9 7 5 3 1

For Owen Dudley Edwards

CONTENTS

ACKNOWLEDGEMENTS

My first thanks are due to the Master and Fellows of Trinity College Cambridge, whose invitation to deliver the Clark Lectures in the Lent term of 2009 was the occasion that produced this book. In particular I am grateful to the hospitality and help extended by the Master, Lord Rees, Boyd Hilton, and Adrian Poole. Other friends in Cambridge, whose support and friendship contributed greatly to ease the rather nerve-racking occasions of the lectures, include Lauren Arrington, John Bew, Eugenio Biagini, Stefan Collini, the late Frank Kermode, Joep Leerssen, Miri Rubin, and Gareth Steadman Jones: I am grateful to them all. For help with various aspects while writing the lectures, and subsequently turning them into a book, I owe much to the help and advice of Eamonn Cantwell, Warwick Gould, Alvin Jackson, Matt Kelly, Ian McBride, Robert Portsmouth, Joseph Rezek, Deirdre Toomey, Sophie Topley, James Wilson, and above all Tom Dunne, Claire Connolly, and Hermione Lee, each of whom read the whole thing and commented trenchantly on it, to my great profit. So did my wife, Aisling, to whom I owe more than I can say. Jules Iddon was a stalwart help in putting the book together, as always going well beyond the call of duty. I must also record my thanks to my agents Gill Coleridge and Cara Jones, for smoothing the way to publication; to my editors at Oxford University Press, Jacqueline Baker and Ariane Petit; to Zoe Spilberg for her help with picture research; and to Donna Poppy, for her characteristically immaculate and penetrating copy-editing and editorial suggestions. The dedication records another debt, to Owen Dudley Edwards, for his unrivalled knowledge of the by-ways of nineteenth-century Irish (and Scottish) literature; it is also a grateful acknowledgement of his friendship and welcome to the Foster family on their various Edinburgh sojourns. He has not, however, read this text, and I alone am responsible for any errors it may contain.

LIST OF ILLUSTRATIONS

INTRODUCTION

The inheritance left to Irish literature, and no less to Irish history, by W. B. Yeats is a subject frequently confronted; it preoccupies many commentators, and affected his literary contemporaries and successors in Ireland. For them, in the words of Austin Clarke, it was like growing up in the shadow of a great oak tree which had sapped all the moisture from the soil and blotted out 'the friendly sun' from the surrounding saplings.[1] The complications and implications of his relationships with other writers, living through a time of historical flux, have been suggested by critics such as Richard Ellmann and Phillip L. Marcus, and form an inextricable part of his biography—which is, as T. S. Eliot long ago remarked, also the story of his times: he was 'part of the consciousness of an age which cannot be understood without him'.[2] One result of Yeats's spectacular imposition upon events and people around him and after him is that what came before tends to take second place, or to be taken for granted: the impact, novelty, and decisiveness of his work, from its early appearance, is regarded as a given. 'All begins in Yeats', as George Moore put it, 'and all ends in Yeats.'[3]

The recent, and welcome, critical and historical attention paid to Irish writing in the early and mid nineteenth century has not changed this emphasis. Even surveys which discuss earlier writers with the object of ending in Yeats's emergence tend to take for granted the idea that he subverts and challenges most of what has gone before[4]—an impression which he himself took considerable care to create in his underestimated critical writings as well as in his autobiographies. Though these profile the growth of a poet's mind with, at times, a Wordsworthian solipsism, a careful reading might suggest an immersion in local literary tradition more reminiscent of Joyce.[5]

The intention of this short book is to return to the fertile seedbed of nineteenth-century Irish writing, and draw out themes which had particular resonance for Yeats (and, to a lesser extent, for the Irish Literary Revival at large). It has been stimulated by a number of individual studies by a range of gifted scholars in the last generation, who have revived interest in forgotten fictions and raised fascinating questions of influence, and my debt to them is obvious in my notes. The format of the Clark Lectures, which I was asked to deliver at Cambridge in the spring of 2009, offered a stimulating and suggestive framework, and the chapters of this book retrace it. Following my theme of Yeats as inheritor, I was also impelled to return to the ideas with which I began my own exploration of his intellectual pedigree, more than twenty years ago—particularly the discussion of occult themes in Irish Victorian writing, the subject of much subsequent attention.[6] The idea that scholars should devote themselves to Yeats's interest in the supernatural was scornfully rejected by a previous Clark Lecturer, F. R. Leavis, in his own 1967 series, published as *English Literature in Our Time and in the University*. Yeats was not Dr Leavis's only target: he was incredulous that a Kingsley Amis novel could be described as a 'serious statement about amorality', dismissed the Open University as an 'exalted and subsidized correspondence college', and warned fiercely about 'American habits of research', making them sound like what used to be called 'Hunnish practices'.[7] But he did also make the point that a historical knowledge of the civilization behind a piece of creative writing enhances our understanding of that work. Historians must be grateful to him for that (even if they cannot agree that *Hard Times* is Dickens's most important novel). And it is apposite for a historian to see Yeats as an inheritor of a nineteenth-century tradition—or a complex of traditions—rather than simply as a creator of literary modernism in the twentieth century.

The picture has always been complicated by Yeats's own commitment to revising his canon—and, along with it, as he thought, remaking himself. Invaluable studies of his poetry collections and plays from manuscript stage onwards show how radically their forms changed; and comparisons of the canonical final volumes to his first publications show how much was jettisoned along the way. The title of this book comes from one of the few very early poems to make the cut and remain, though much rewritten, in the body of his *Collected Poems*—where it appears as the very first poem in the first section, titled 'The Song of the Happy Shepherd'. It was first published in the *Dublin University Review* in October 1885, when Yeats was twenty. In the earliest version, the speaker argues against abstract study, since truth only resides 'in thine own heart'.

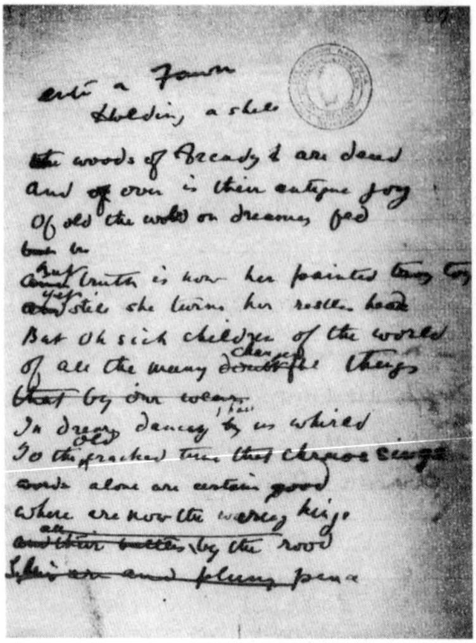

FIGURE I Manuscript draft of 'The Happy Shepherd' by W. B. Yeats, early 1880s

Go gather by the humming sea
Some twisted, echo-harbouring shell
And to its lips thy story tell,
And they thy comforters will be,
Rewording in melodious guile,
Thy fretful words a little while,
Till they shall singing fade in ruth
For ruth and joy have brotherhood,
And words alone are certain good,
Sing then, for this is also sooth.[8]

The style and expression of the young Victorian Yeats would change almost beyond recognition from the point when this poem was written. This book attempts to chart some of the influences that created the original and powerful Yeatsian voice of the decade from 1885 to 1895, a voice which would itself go through many alterations from the *fin de siècle* until his death in 1939. But throughout all the changes and variations imposed on this particular early poem by its protean author, the penultimate line of this stanza remained: 'words alone are certain good'. Some years after Yeats's death, Louis MacNeice, discussing the great poet with Thomas Sturge Moore, agreed that this line represented 'a text from which he never swerved'.[9] It may be glossed as an invitation to escapism, ironically suggested at a point just before his own involvement in nationalist politics through the Young Ireland societies of the mid 1880s. But, more profoundly, it may also suggest that ultimate truths are located and preserved in stories, traditions, and legends, rather than in theories or dogma—and that poetry can enshrine them.

In another mood, Yeats would later recall that his own critical writings of the 1880s led towards manufacturing unreal propaganda, involving him in 'unrealities and half-truths'. 'All one's life one struggles towards reality, finding always but new veils. One knows everything in one's mind. It is the words, children of the occasion, that betray.'[10] He would return to the thought that the 'words' of literary tradition should be freed from the excess political baggage with which so many Irish nineteenth-century writers were freighted—first by opponents in their own day, and subsequently by present-minded commentators in later eras. To read these writers, Yeats's predecessors, in their full and complex contexts, reimagining contemporary preoccupations and implications, cross-referencing them to the realities that surrounded

FIGURE 2 W. B. Yeats in 1886 by J. B. Yeats

and linked them, can help convey what Yeats absorbed from them. I want to indicate a few of the ways this might be done by considering the suggestive mix of politics, poetry, journalism, and supernatural themes in Irish nineteenth-century writing, with the eventual aim of seeing Yeats's emergence from this background. But the bulk of this book is concerned with the traditions of Irish literature that lie behind him, rather than with his own work.

Thus it begins by looking at Irish writing in the early years of the Anglo-Irish Union of 1800, and its interpretation—at the time and since. The intention is to consider nationalism, Romanticism, and—loosely—Celticism in its literary manifestations; to query how far a 'national tale', in the nineteenth-century formulation, is necessarily a nationalist one; to revisit the complex literary enterprise of the mid-century Young Ireland movement, a looming presence for the literary nationalists of the *fin de siècle*; to explore themes of the Gothic and the supernatural in the nineteenth-century Irish consciousness; to indicate something about readerships, influences, and intentions—authorial intentions, that is, rather than the intentions imposed later on by ingenious critics. And eventually to consider the emergence of a 'national' poet, if not quite a nationalist bard, by the 1890s, and discuss W. B. Yeats as the recipient and interrogator of a rich and involved, if often misinterpreted, literary tradition, which in fact formed the subject of his own neglected early critical writings. His literary persona derived from this conditioning as well as from his status as a great avatar of twentieth-century modernism, though of course he was that as well. Rereading Yeats's early work in the light of these influences suggests that we may have underestimated the extent to which themes of continuity as much as discontinuity inflect Irish literary history—as they do other Irish histories.

1

National Tales and National Futures in Ireland and Scotland after 1800

I

In 1897 the acute Irish critic Stephen Gwynn (himself a budding politician as well as writer) remarked:

Literature in Ireland... is almost inextricably connected with considerations foreign to art: it is regarded as a means, not as an end. During the nineteenth century the belief being general among all classes of Irish people that the English knew nothing of Ireland, every book on an Irish subject was judged by the effect it was likely to have upon English opinion to which the Irish are naturally sensitive, since it decides the most important Irish questions. But apart from this practical aspect of the matter, there is a morbid national sensitiveness which desires to be consulted. Ireland, though she ought to count herself amply justified of her children, is still complaining that she is misunderstood among the nations; she is forever crying out for someone to give her keener sympathy, fuller appreciation, and exhibit herself and her grievances to the world in a true light. The result is that kind of insincerity and special pleading which has been the curse of Irish or Anglo-Irish literature. I write of a literature which has its natural centre in Dublin, not Connemara; which looks eastward, not westward.[1]

As Gwynn suggests, Irish imaginative writing in the nineteenth century was seen as actively and instinctively 'political'. By the time he was writing—the 1890s—Irish literature was entering its celebrated 'Revival' or 'Renaissance'. As part of this reassessment, the fiction of the early nineteenth century had become the material for anthologies, and the assumptions behind it were being discussed energetically by a new generation of nationalist critic: notably Gwynn's contemporary, the young W. B. Yeats. The inheritance which this particular Revivalist took from his forerunners is one theme of this chapter; another is the political interpretation applied to the fiction of the early nineteenth century, and its parallels with Scottish writing in the same era.

Scottish echoes are also raised by Gwynn's accusation that nineteenth-century Irish novelists wrote for England rather than Ireland. This theme would recur more pointedly in the influential nationalist literary critique of Daniel Corkery in the 1930s, and later still in the highly suggestive work of Seamus Deane. It also lies behind Joep Leerssen's witty definition 'auto-exoticism', which describes the way that Irish writers present their country as bizarre, *sui generis*, 'other', even to themselves: 'looking for one's own identity in the unusual, the extraordinary, the exotic aspects of experience, to conflate the notions of one's distinctness and one's distinctiveness. Irish history, as a result, tends to be traced back to mythical, fictional but colourful roots; Irish life tends to be reduced to its un-English aspects.'[2] It reflects, too, the way that literary history has come to be seen in the light of intended audiences and readers' responses as well as the hybrid nature of culture in the Irish and British nineteenth-century world. This is relevant to the literary movement which Yeats dominated at the end of the nineteenth century. But it is worth beginning with issues of politicization in Irish writing in the decades after the Union—and with critical interpretations over the last few years, which are politicized in their own way.

Just after the Act of Union in 1800, a flood of novels appeared from Irish writers who advanced an agenda of moral improvement as well as literary entertainment; they also advocated

FIGURE 3   Maria Edgeworth

FIGURE 4 Sydney Owenson
[Lady Morgan] by Daniel
Maclise

historical enlightenment and adopted an allegorical bent.[3] The
most prominent were Maria Edgeworth and Sydney Owenson
(also known as Lady Morgan), author of *The Wild Irish Girl* and
much else, but the genre can be extended to take in the Banim
brothers, Gerald Griffin, and many more obscure names—creating works which blended fictional fantasy with lectures upon
Irish history and allegorical commentary on the state of the
country. This set a tone which would characterize Irish fiction
for much of the nineteenth century. The phenomenon did not
spring from nothing; these writers were clearly influenced by
eighteenth-century developments in the aesthetic of the novel,
notably the 1790s 'novel of ideas'.[4] But the Irish fiction of the

4

early 1800s is *sui generis* nonetheless. The plots of books such as Edgeworth's *The Absentee* and *Ormond*, Owenson's *The Wild Irish Girl* and (far superior) *The O'Briens and the O'Flahertys*, Charles Maturin's *The Milesian Chief*, not to mention a host of forgotten texts such as William Parnell's *Maurice and Berghetta* (1819), may vary in verisimilitude, economy of effect, and readability, but striking elements of similarity remain. A young hero, bred outside Ireland but usually with an ancestral Irish connection, travels westward and undergoes a process of education. He is exposed to a gallery of Irish types: archaic chieftain, faithful servant, authentic aristocrat, self-interested collaborator, imitative social climber, Continental exile, self-destructive revolutionary, and above all an Irishwoman who educates him through love. The politics of violence usually hover in the background, and are usually evaded; at the end resolution comes in the form of emigration for some (the irreconcilable or the ineducable), agricultural improvement for others, and a symbolic marriage for the principals. 'Union' may be the desideratum, but Irish history looms behind everything, as ominous and omnipresent as the Western mountain ranges. Ironically, one of the chief reasons why these themes nowadays strike such a familiar note lies outside Ireland: it is because Walter Scott used these Irish models so liberally in *Waverley* and elsewhere. And elements of these fictions can also be detected in *The Speckled Bird*, the unfinished novel which Yeats embarked upon in 1897 just as Gwynn delivered his judgement about the 'special pleading' of Irish literature.

The profusion and popularity of this literature raised enduring questions for Irish critics such as Gwynn (not to mention Deane), much as Scott's pre-eminence created problems for later generations of Scottish nationalists. Moreover, in recent years this genre has become something of a political football in Irish studies, especially in terms of the construction of nationalism. There is an argument for reclaiming these works on behalf of historians, and attempting to see them in the context of their times. This has indeed been suggested by some Irish historians, notably Oliver MacDonagh and Tom Dunne. But early-nine-teenth-century Irish fiction might be related not only to strik-ing developments in the prominence and authority of women writers, but also to a world of literary production which takes in Scotland as well as Ireland—setting the scene for a 'politics of Irish literature' which projects forward into the mid nineteenth century and beyond.[5]

There are other varieties of politicization. In his influ-ential book *Strange Country* Seamus Deane sees the whole question of nineteenth-century Irish writing as a highly structured 'paradigm' for the opposing political projects of Unionism and nationalism—an analysis that culminates in a denunciation of late-twentieth-century Irish historians for collud-ing in and advancing 'the Unionist project'. (Like that cheerful phrase 'the Enlightenment project', this may assume rather more than the circumstances merit.) Other literary-historical critics, staying more closely with the matter in hand, have approached the fiction of the early nineteenth century in terms of contemporary theories of the stadial development of society from barbarism to civility, and anticipations of post-colonialism.[6] These approaches, stimulating as they are, tend to downplay the fact that the 'project' advanced by Owenson, the Banims, and others is not national-ism but Catholic Emancipation—though it must be accepted that subversive allegorical arguments lie beneath many of these texts of superficial reconciliation. On another level of subversion, the fractured and offbeat Irish fictions of the early nineteenth century are sometimes seen as anticipations of twentieth-century Irish modernism, not as awkward provincial variants of a contemporary English model.[7] Like Irish furniture or Irish architecture of the period, their deviations indicate sophistication, not faroucheness. It is a nice idea, but raises another kind of anachronism.

More profitably, the didactic novels of Edgeworth, Owenson, the Banims, and Maturin have been challengingly analysed by Katie Trumpener, Ina Ferris, Claire Connolly, and others in terms of the conventions of myth, epic, and national tale.[8] This also raises the question of the cultural formation of nationalism, and the part played therein by the development of novel-writing—leading to the creation of that shared imagination and shared reading audience by which national communities are imagined. Or so we have been taught by Benedict Anderson, a great analyst of nationalism who is, incidentally, Irish.[9] The business of 'placing' Irish literature, so familiar to Stephen Gwynn, Daniel Corkery, and their contemporaries, has over the last generation become once more a preoccupation. Literary history has been politicized and polemicized all over again, reliving the controversies that greeted the first publication of the key novel of Romantic Irish reclamation, Owenson's *The Wild Irish Girl*. Published in 1806, the story of the aristocratic Horatio, whose travels in Connacht bring him into the exotic world of the Prince of Inismore and his harpist daughter Glorvina, supplied the model whereby an innocent hero begins by discovering wild Ireland and ends by contracting a symbolic marriage to a bride who epitomizes her country.

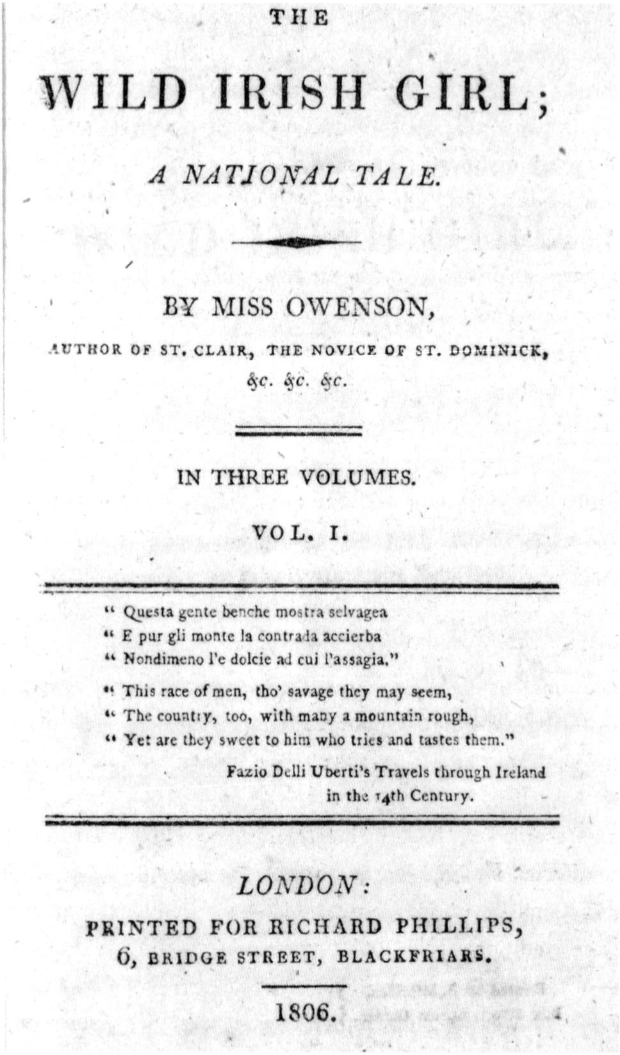

THE

WILD IRISH GIRL;

A NATIONAL TALE.

———◆———

BY MISS OWENSON,

AUTHOR OF ST. CLAIR, THE NOVICE OF ST. DOMINICK,
&c. &c. &c.

IN THREE VOLUMES.

VOL. I.

" Questa gente benche mostra selvagea
" E pur gli monte la contrada accierba
" Nondimeno l'e dolcie ad cui l'assagia."

" This race of men, tho' savage they may seem,
" The country, too, with many a mountain rough,
" Yet are they sweet to him who tries and tastes them."

Fazio Delli Uberti's Travels through Ireland
in the 14th Century.

LONDON:

PRINTED FOR RICHARD PHILLIPS,
6, BRIDGE STREET, BLACKFRIARS.

1806.

FIGURE 5 Title page of first edition of *The Wild Irish Girl*, 1806

The ostensible argument for education, improvement, and reconciliation, however, nowadays does not seem so simple. Psychoanalysing the literary imagination, some have interpreted Ireland as 'England's unconscious'—a monstrous secret history lurking in the guilty subconscious of 'endemically idealist England'.[10] Nineteenth-century Irish fictions are interpreted principally as symptoms of political crisis, in a way that would not have surprised Gwynn. Perhaps more productively, the notion of a generic Irish Romanticism, prospected some time ago by Tom Dunne but left rather unattended, has moved back into the picture. This has complicated and enriched our understanding of what is loosely termed 'national literature' in the early nineteenth century, as has Emer Nolan's suggestive readings of Catholic novelists after Moore.[11] And very recently the notion of a comparative literary history focused on Ireland and Scotland has inspired some seminal and exciting work, reaching well beyond counterfactual speculations as to why Ireland never produced a *Waverley*, or why Scotland did not have a nationalist revolution. This perspective owes a good deal to developments in historiography rather than in literary criticism, particularly those instigated by J. G. A. Pocock in analysing Britishness; it may also reflect a movement within English studies away from literary theory and towards literary history. And it has recently been affected and conditioned by the rediscovery of a profuse Irish fictional literature from the eighteenth century, overturning the traditional idea that *Castle Rackrent* neatly marks the start of the Union with the first Anglo-Irish novel.[12]

Thus the way that the history of Irish literature is currently interpreted has been resolutely and often excitingly politicized.

And a similar process is happening in Scottish literature, for reasons that must have something to do with recent and current political developments.[13] It may not be too much to say that both phenomena owe much to the revival of nationalism, which in some quarters seems to be returning to the status of primordial urge rather than imaginative construct. It may be, however, that the fiction of the early nineteenth century in Ireland and Scotland needs to be read in the light not only of latent or proto-nationalism, but of experimental Unionism—which is what meant most to the writers actually producing it.

II

For the cultural condition of Ireland in the early nineteenth century may not have been as unique as sometimes supposed, and Scottish parallels and influences came easily to contemporary minds. There was a certain amount of previous history here. The wars over James Macpherson's publication of so-called Ossianic poetic 'fragments' in the mid eighteenth century raised at once the question of how far these re-invented myths of Fingal and company were lifted from Irish sources: the debate is rehearsed by the characters of Owenson's *Wild Irish Girl* as well as in Scott's *The Antiquary*, and incensed eighteenth-century Irish scholars immersed in their own discoveries of a native epic literary tradition.[14] The controversy simmered on well into the nineteenth century, until Yeats deliberately recolonized this very territory for Ireland in 1889 with his first poetic epic, *The Wanderings of Oisin*. Indeed, it may not be over yet.[15] Remaining with the early nineteenth century, it is worth emphasizing, first, the popularity and influence of creative literature produced in the Celtic realms, and, second, the connections and comparisons between the literary worlds of Ireland and Scotland, Dublin and Edinburgh—since this casts a rather different light on Irish productions too readily seen as existing in some marginal and exoticized limbo.

The novels produced for avid and profitable Irish and Scottish markets in the early 1800s took contested history as their theme, in ways that were at once similar and oddly contrasting; there is also an implicit cross-channel dialogue between some of the most celebrated fictions of the era. Of course, the circumstances are different: the commentaries produced in Scotland are evaluating a century of fairly profitable union with England, whereas Ireland was just setting out on the same course with consequences that were fairly disastrous. The Irish Union got off to a bad start with a broken promise: Catholic Emancipation. This exercised every didactic Irish imagination. Civil rights for Catholics had been a supposed condition of Union; it remained the unfinished business, the 'national cause' adverted to by writers such as Owenson, the Banims, and Thomas Moore. 'My romances', wrote Owenson in old age, 'were not written merely to amuse the reader. They were written *for* and *in* the great cause of *Catholic Emancipation*, the theme and inspiration of my early authorship and the conviction of my after life.'[16] This emancipation would not come, grudgingly, till 1829: its withholding created the terms of Irish politics in the first third of the nineteenth century, and arguably till much later.

Thus the relationship between religious profession and political identity provided a ready issue for comparison and contrast between Ireland and Scotland. Opening his great history of Ireland in the eighteenth century, W. E. H. Lecky optimistically claimed that eighteenth-century Scottish history furnished 'one of the most remarkable instances on record of the efficacy of wise legislation in developing the prosperity and ameliorating the character of nations', whereas the history of Ireland in the eighteenth century demonstrated 'with singular clearness the perverting and degrading influence of great legislative injustices and the manner in which they affect in turn every element of national well-being'.[17] In the age of Home Rule the same point was made by many other historians and pundits (Justin McCarthy, William Law Mathieson, Albert Venn Dicey), but the argument was by then a venerable one. Robert Southey pointed the

FIGURE 6 Calton Hill, Edinburgh, by J. M. W. Turner, 1820

FIGURE 7 Christ's Cathedral, Dublin, by George Petrie, 1820

same contrast in 1810,[18] and the Irish novelists of the era would
have said no different. Contemporary sets of engravings show it
vividly. Edinburgh is delineated as the new Athens, while Dublin
is portrayed as the location of gloomy ruins. As the nineteenth
century wore on, it became clearer and clearer that Scotland
won out against the other Celtic realms: the Caledonian stereo-
type hardy, successful, and bracingly beautiful, while the Welsh
were seen as mendacious, hypocritical, and sexually incontinent,
and the Irish brutish, stupid, dirty, and disloyal. In fact, early-
nineteenth-century Scotland no less than Ireland was marked by
endemic poverty, epic drinking, traumatic emigration, brutal violence, and a history of dispossession. Nonetheless Scotland the
Brave emerged as a jewel of Empire, turning out bonny, brainy,
humorous empire-builders; 'Scotty' the resourceful engineer

endured all the way to *Star Trek*. Protestantism of course has a lot to do with it. But the Scots also kept vital freedoms in education and the law as well as religion, enjoyed an industrial revolution at the right time, and infiltrated metropolitan government.

Early-nineteenth-century Scottish culture was also, as they say, coming from somewhere else. Historical analysis today might be less sunny about the universal success story of eighteenth-century Scotland, especially with Jacobitism currently at the forefront of historiographical fashion. At the moment, emphasis also falls on the disparities of wealth created by the economic efflorescence of the era, and its basis in various forms of exploitation (including slavery). But whatever the fate of Highland society, the brilliance of eighteenth-century intellectual life in the Lowlands remains and forms the necessary backdrop to the emergent genius of Walter Scott. The other great literary influence of the early nineteenth century, Byron, has audaciously been claimed for Scotland too, a process that began with Byron's Irish friend and biographer, Tom Moore. Scottish aesthetic models were immensely important in defining the emerging category of polite literature. But Byron, and Scott the novelist, burst on a literary scene that was already dominated by Irish bestsellers, notably Maria Edgeworth and Moore himself, as well as Sydney Owenson.

In 1814 Scott's landmark novel *Waverley* nodded not only specifically to Edgeworth but also covertly to Owenson's *Wild Irish Girl*, a publishing sensation at exactly the point, eight years before, when Scott began the abandoned outline of his first novel. Famously, in his general introduction to the Waverley novels, Scott gave full credit to Edgeworth for having inspired him to attempt a local fiction, but he did not mention the less respectable Owenson—though Peter Garside's magisterial work on the origins of *Waverley* places her firmly in the frame of inspirational reference.[19] Edgeworth, a bluestocking Irish Ascendancy intellectual and educationalist, had by then produced a string of bestsellers, several with Irish themes, though it is *Castle Rackrent* in 1800 for which she is nowadays remembered. In this brilliantly elliptical unreliable-narrator fiction, a faithful retainer (or is he?) charts the decline and fall of a ramshackle Irish family. Though landlords, they are of old Irish stock, and are observed with an offhand sarcasm which still scorches the page. In each generation the Rackrents throw up an inadequate scion, referred to with a kind of dismissive familiarity (Sir Kit, Sir Condy) by the narrator Thady Quirke—while his own son, Jason, a rising attorney, moves in from the margins to take over the estate. Successive marriages, debts, rows, duels, affrays are retailed in a series of deadpan asides; the texture is apparently thinner than Edgeworth's other Irish novels, *The Absentee* and *Ormond*, and the message less openly didactic, but its social and historical inferences are all the more vivid for that.

This, too, recalls Scott. Reading Edgeworth, or Owenson, or Tom Moore—the heady combination of historical and sociological and even anthropological underpinning (sometimes in footnote form), the use of Gaelic poetry and ballads, and above all the shaping of creative literature to interrogate a contested and recently traumatic history—obvious thematic links arise. Scott's access to a sophisticated tradition of philosophical and sociological analysis may have helped him towards the pattern of reconciliation with the past and the realistic acceptance of change, which infuses his particular Romanticism with his own conservative irony. This has echoes in Edgeworth's later novels, and less expectedly in Owenson's *The O'Briens and the O'Flahertys*. Though the uses of Irish history were superficially less amenable to Scott-like reconciliations, Edgeworth at least has not been given her due as an analyst of a new society in the making. Her writings have been suggestively interpreted as a symptom of colonial consciousness; the themes of 'improvement' and the education of a colonial elite which pervade *The Absentee* may seem to bear this out. At the same time, the story of young Lord Colambre, who rejects both his father's Irish fecklessness and his mother's obsession with appearing 'a Henglishwoman born and bred', in order to learn about Ireland on something like its own terms, suggests Scottish parallels. Similarly, his courtship of his supposed cousin Grace Nugent enables negotiation with an aristocratic Irish tradition which turns out not to be what it seems. On many levels, it is more enlightening to read Edgeworth's fiction in terms of envisioning an Irish future on the Scottish model.[20]

This is especially true of the underrated *Ormond* (1817), with its theme of an easily tempted young hero exploring archaic Gaelic values posited against the expanding Hanoverian state.[21] But the preface to *Castle Rackrent* may be instanced too. 'When Ireland loses her identity by an union with Great Britain, she will look back with a smile of good-humoured complacency on the Sir Kits and Sir Condys of her former existence.' The concept of 'loss of identity' itself requires some ironic decoding, as does Edgeworth's preceding throwaway remark that 'nations, as well as individuals, gradually lose attachment to their identity'.[22] Again, Edgeworth might be seen as sceptical and slightly perverse in her engagement with the irrational and intractable forces of Irish history, rather than as a didactic colonial social engineer. Walter Scott might agree: an implicit correspondence can be discerned between his *Redgauntlet*, written 1823–4, and Edgeworth's *Ormond*, published six years earlier. In both novels young men in search of father-figures explore the peripheries of their disputed nation. Darsie Latimer, riding around the debatable lands of the Solway Firth, echoes Harry Ormond's voyage to the Black Islands off the Connemara coast. These Romantic heroes, weak-willed and too good-looking for their own good, are helped in their quest for heredity by older women, and in both cases the necessity of improving the intractable landscape presents a powerful theme. In both novels, too, the old order is represented by a glamorous but archaic father-figure: the charismatic but ill-tempered Laird of Redgauntlet and the unworldly but morally upright King Corny. Both Scott and Edgeworth, like Owenson slightly before them, face questions of historical authenticity, and the derivation or usurpation of rights and authority with the coming of a new order.[23] There is also a subtler engagement with the questions left hanging by a rebellious history and its extinction than either is sometimes credited with: in *Waverley, Ormond,* and *The O'Briens and the O'Flahertys*, Scott, Edgeworth, and Owenson portray those Irish and Scots who curry favour with the Hanoverian state as dislikeable trimmers. A shared history of violence is linked to a seductive if outmoded ideology.

When Scott toured parts of Ireland with Edgeworth in 1825, he reassured himself that 'the Irish are no more the Irish of 1797 [*recte* 1798] than the Scotch are the Scotch of 1745', but in some ways 1745 and 1798 are not so very far apart.[24] This visit was the culmination of a long preoccupation: he had long wanted to edit Swift, and to write a novel about the Irish rebel Redmond O'Hanlon. Visiting the country, he referred to the 'severe oppression' of the Irish, second only to the injustice borne by West Indian blacks: and, similarly, Scott reflected that their obdurate cheerfulness was 'the saddest feature of the whole story'.[25] (As with Carlyle, the stereotypical view of Scott is set rather askew by his reactions to actual Irish people.) Scott nonetheless believed in 1825 that 'everything is mending', while simultaneously contributing cheerfully to the view of 'national character' already being enshrined by travelogues as well as novels.[26] 'I never saw a richer country or, to speak my mind, a finer people; the worst of them is the bitter and envenomed dislike they have to each other.' He also observed: 'They are certainly a very odd people, and but for that ugly humour of murdering, which is in full decline, they would be the most amusing and easy to live with in the world.'[27] Scott valued amusingness, a quality in which he thought Highlanders were sadly deficient; he even managed to kiss the Blarney Stone while in Ireland, which supposedly confers entertaining eloquence (hardly lacking in his case). But there are more profound correspondences too. Clare O'Halloran has pointed out that the issues of debate pursued in *The Antiquary* raise close Irish parallels in terms of origin legends, settlement, and displacement, while Garside has noted marked assonances between Owenson's *O'Donnel* (1814) and Scott's *The Bride of Lammermoor* (1819).[28] And another Irish novel which *Redgauntlet* 'answers' quite strikingly is Charles Maturin's *Melmoth the Wanderer* of 1820: Darsie's discovery that he is of Redgauntlet's family, physically marked by

FIGURE 8 Walter Scott kissing the Blarney Stone on his Irish tour in 1825

the same indentation in his forehead and possibly by more sinister birthmarks still, echoes John Melmoth's discovery of his own relationship to a wicked uncle, deeply implicated in the corrupt bargains of Irish history. Since Scott knew Maturin, corresponded with him, advised him, and even lent him money, such cross-fertilization is not improbable; similar patterns can be traced between Maturin's *The Milesian Chief* and *The Bride of Lammermoor*. *Melmoth*, with its bargains, family hatreds, and doppelgängers, may be echoed in another Scots classic of this era, James Hogg's *The Private Memoirs and Confessions of a Justified Sinner*, published the same year as *Redgauntlet*. And those critics who see Irish early-nineteenth-century fiction as peculiarly *sui generis* and proto-modernist in its use of spoof footnotes, made-up epigraphs, manipulation of eccentric voices, and narrative in-jokes have clearly forgotten Scott's *Antiquary*, which epitomizes all these tricks and stratagems.

There is more to say about Scottish and Irish interminglings projected through the protean figure of Scott. Two years after publishing *Redgauntlet*, he began the series of 'Malachi Malagrowther' articles, inspired by the proposal to abolish Scotland's separate currency and modelled on Swift's *Drapier's Letters*. Appearing in the *Edinburgh Weekly Journal* in 1826, this manifesto proposed a 'friendly alliance' between Ireland and Scotland as a counterweight to centralizing English ambitions. (The Irish Exchequer had been abolished in 1817, a late result of the Act of Union.) The language Scott puts in Malachi's mouth sits oddly with the reductionist version of his political views as a Tory Unionist:

> Now, what say you to a league offensive and defensive, against all such measures as tend to the suppression of any just right belonging to either country, in virtue of the Articles of Union respectively?...John Bull is, not unnaturally, desirous of having rather more than his own share in managing the great national coach-and-six...let us remain as Nature made us, Englishmen, Irishmen and Scotchmen, with something of the impress of our several countries upon each.[29]

Latter-day Scottish critics of a nationalist inclination suggestively emphasize the impact of Scott's work on nascent European nationalities (Hungary, Catalonia, Bohemia, Slovenia, Italy) and discern 'national feeling' as affecting Scott more in his later years.[30] Recent criticism has taken it further by stating roundly that Scottish Romanticism and Irish Romanticism have to be read 'as distinct national entities pursuing discrete literary strategies', and that in Scott's case his work must be read 'against Polish, Czech, Hungarian and French Romanticism' rather than in a 'four-nations' British context. This is stimulating stuff, appealing to the cultural historian, but it does not quite square with what Scott thought he was doing and Malachi Malagrowther might not agree with it.[31] Proto-nationalism does not always convince as the cement bonding Scots–Irish connections in this era; but it may be enlightening to see them in terms of adaptations of, as well as to, Unionism.

Reading Walter Scott in context, the Irish parallels and connections are striking. The close correspondence (in every sense) with Edgeworth means more than Scott straightforwardly following her example and eclipsing her; this leaves out both Scott's real and continuing interest in Ireland, and Edgeworth's enormous contemporary popularity, now forgotten. Her reputation nowadays rests on *Castle Rackrent*, an oddly modern, fractured, satirical story, replete with in-jokes and ironies, which looks back to Sterne as much as forward to Molly Keane (or even Flann O'Brien). Hibernocentric critics tend to forget that her next novel, *Belinda*, had nothing to do with Ireland (and earned her three times as much money). Her reputation in feminist literary history highlights her approach to economics and her interpretation of forms of domesticity—aspects of her work not often seen in apposition to its 'Irish' content, except by Cliona Ó Gallchoir.[32] Indeed, some commentary on Edgeworth's Irish 'national tales' addresses them with an oddly personalized venom. She has been variously stigmatized by recent Irish critics as an 'effete Whig', 'English-provincial in a Protestant tradition', and an aggressive colonist peddling 'a genteel version of old plantation policies'.[33]

This presumably means the agricultural-improvement themes of *The Absentee*, but it is less easy to apply this dismissive judgement to *Ennui*, much less *Ormond*, where the hero implicitly opts for Gaelic feudal ties in the end, taking over King Corny's role in the Black Islands. And even *The Absentee* argues powerfully for affirming an Irish 'identity' by living at home and abjuring superficial English fashions.

As for *Castle Rackrent*, Deane more convincingly sees it as a demonstration that the eighteenth-century Scottish theories of aesthetics, sensibility, and economics, which prepared the way for Walter Scott's projection of reconciliation with the past, just do not apply in Ireland. Edgeworth, Deane says, was trying to apply 'a fictional convention that had evolved in England for other purposes', without a viable theory of society behind it.[34] Irish Romantic literature, from this point of view, 'could form no articulation with social or political philosophy'. Though there is a certain predeterminism at work here, and perhaps a slightly mechanical view of the novelist's business, it corresponds with de Tocqueville's thoughtful 1835 comparison of how aristocratic authority worked in England, and failed in Ireland: 'The two societies...were...both founded on the principle of aristocracy. The two aristocracies of which I have been speaking, have the same origin and manners and almost the same laws. But the one has for centuries given the English one of the best governments that exist in the world; the other has given the Irish one of the most detestable that could ever be imagined.'[35] Deane is equally astute in locating the chronological time-frame so carefully delineated by Edgeworth for her tale of dissolute landlords, faithful if bewildered servants, and rising agents. She specifically places the action before 1782 (the achievement of partial autonomy under 'Grattan's Parliament') and, in the preface and elsewhere, exercises retrospective authorial judgement on the eve of the Act of Union in 1800. Thus far, so political. Traditional 'feeling' is posited against the modernizing forces of historical process.

But is this novel a work of 'startling incoherence', written by someone who is incapable of seeing Irish society as other than hopelessly 'pathological', and therefore takes refuge in whimsy and opaqueness?[36] The accompanying implication is that Scottish conditions allow 'an end to history' and a reconciliation with the modern state but Irish conditions do not, because there, 'history is not yet finished': a distinctly teleological view of the doomed Union. And so, in Deane's view, alcoholism becomes the necessary allegorical end of the individual story instead of marriage. This is how he interprets the last cryptic sentence of Edgeworth's startling commentary in *Castle Rackrent*, inserted by 'the Editor' after Thady signs off. 'Did the Warwickshire militia, who were chiefly artisans, teach the Irish to drink beer, or did they learn from the Irish to drink whiskey?' It is certainly a strange ending to a strange novel: Edgeworth suddenly slews into the rhetorical mode of Bishop Berkeley's *Querist*, with a surreal non sequitur worthy of Myles na Gopaleen. But her question may be whether the end-point of English–Irish cultural interaction works out as a levelling up, or a levelling down. How does reconciliation work?

The notion that Irish history in the early nineteenth century was incapable of being 'finished' by reconciliation seems to beg some questions, and to make some assumptions dependent on hindsight. Certainly, the question why things happened differently in Scotland pulses below many of these considerations—just as

Irish conditions preoccupied many Scots intellectuals of the age. (Carlyle, again, looms on the horizon.) The early years of the *Edinburgh Review* (founded in 1802) saw a succession of weighty articles on Ireland—principally on the need for Catholic Eman- cipation, and on the security problem presented by a disaffected Ireland during the French Wars, but also on Irish travel litera- ture, Irish fiction, and Irish oratory.[37] The *Edinburgh* also took an 'Irish' line by continuing to ridicule the Ossian myth, calling for scholarly investigation into authentic Irish saga literature, and jeering at the pretensions of Highland forgeries. The most frequent commentators were Francis Jeffrey and Sidney Smith (who wrote, *inter alia*, a major essay on Maria and Richard Lovell Edgeworth's 'Essay on Irish Bulls'). Thomas Moore also appeared in their pages as a commentator as well as a subject for review, publishing in 1826 a major statement on Irish novel-writing. 'At present', he asserted, 'Ireland bids fair to be the great mart of fiction.'[38] This was in default of a national poetic epic:

> It is often asked why no poet of Ireland has yet drawn from her annals a great National subject for his Muse—but they must be ig- norant of the wretched history of that country who ask that ques- tion. Nationality, in the Anglo-Irish Dictionary, means treason— and, unluckily, has had no other meaning for the last six hundred years. That spirit of resistance to England, which in Scotland was loyalty and patriotism, has, in Ireland, always been rebellion. What then is left for the Irish poet?—the Conquerors of his coun- try he will not celebrate, and he rebels he dare not, if he could.

However, the novelist could revel in such rich materials as the 'low, circumventing cunning' of the populace and the 'thoughtless

FIGURE 9 Tom Moore by Daniel Maclise

and tasteless extravagance' of the gentry, making up the 'great concert of discord that reigns throughout' Ireland. National characteristics, once again.

Though this suggests that Moore was thinking of *Castle Rackrent*, his own *Memoirs of Captain Rock* demonstrates that he was well aware of the potential for political allegory that this implied. Its influence, as Emer Nolan has shown, would project forward into future fictions.[39] His readers would have picked up the Edgeworth reference: she was a favourite of the *Edinburgh Review*, where Jeffrey's lengthy and admiring reviews of her novels helped to establish her reputation in Scottish intellectual life, and much of her impressive intellectual armoury had been assembled through a close reading of Scottish enlightenment philosophy, economics, and sociology (Dugald Stewart no less

than Adam Smith).[40] Jeffrey saw the Edgeworth project, inter-
estingly, as a distinctly patriotic one, determined to convey her
affection for Ireland to a British audience and thereby to suggest
ameliorative measures for a 'magnificent country' that had been
sorely misgoverned. (James Mackintosh, also in the *Edinburgh
Review*, followed Scott in comparing the degrading operation of
civil disabilities upon Irish Catholics to the colour bar in the colonies.[41]) If Ireland was 'inferior in civilization', as Sidney Smith
roundly stated, the fault, 'with such a climate, such a soil, and
such a people', could only be 'directly chargeable to the long
wickedness of the English government'.[42] And time and again in
the *Edinburgh*'s pages, Scotland was adduced as a comparison—
notably in the treatment of non-Anglicans, since the enlightened and expedient treatment of Presbyterianism in Scotland
had produced 'loyalty, tranquillity and security' instead of making it 'the seat of rebellion'.[43] Again, the celebration of the civic
environment drove home the message. Yet, looking back into
Scottish history, parallels could be made with equal force.

Nonetheless, the writers of the *Edinburgh Review* tended to
take refuge in nostrums of 'national character' which owed a
good deal to the fiction of Edgeworth and others, and echoed
Walter Scott's Irish impressions. Sidney Smith thought that
Irish character had helped retard improvements—bravery, wit,
generosity, open-heartedness were counterbalanced by van-
ity, extravagance, irascibility, indebtedness, and impatience
with the restraints of law. 'Such a people are not likely to keep
their eyes steadily upon the main chance, like the Scotch or the
Dutch.'[44] Self-critical Irish commentators were capable of playing the same tune, including Isaac Butt, and the marginally Irish

William Hazlitt. Hazlitt saw Irish eloquence as a rhetoric 'born in impulse', whereas Scots eloquence was born of 'mechanism': luxurious extravagance versus rigid formality. In similar mode, the year after de Tocqueville despairingly toured Ireland, the young Tory *littérateur* Isaac Butt, son of a Donegal rector, vilified Irish patriotism as marked by drunken windiness, while Scots nationality took the path of quiet commitment.

> Patriotism will do for a ballad, a toast after dinner, or an apostrophe in a speech—for anything but action. An allusion to 'the emerald isle' at a public meeting will draw thunders of applause...but in that cheap tribute to sentiment, our nationality too often effervesces. Had we half the nationality of Scotchmen, our country would not be as it is. The Irishman will praise his country, but the Scotchman will labour that she may deserve the praise of the world...Irish [nationality] finds its expression in the pathetic poetry of pining sentiment, or in the noisy ebullition of convivial mirth; [Scottish nationality] is exhibited in persevering, sober and business like exertion. The Scotchman cultivates his thistle in his garden; the Irishman wears his shamrock till it withers on his bosom, or he drowns it in his bowl.[45]

We are back with the identity that Edgeworth believed the Irish ought to lose, and the supposedly desirable Scots alternative. The *Edinburgh Review*'s determination to market and comment upon Irish fiction represents an early instance of what Joep Leerssen has seen as the quintessentially nineteenth-century belief that 'literary history is a form of studying the nation's true character as expressed in its cultural history'.[46] The underlying objective was to explain why Scott's and Edgeworth's enterprises came out at different conclusions.

Of course, a more literal political message could be read from the agendas presented in fiction. Hazlitt famously pointed out that Scott, 'in restoring the claims of the Stuarts by courtesy of romance', saw to it that 'the House of Brunswick are more firmly seated in point of fact'.[47] But there are subtler messages, too, in the way that a novel like Edgeworth's *Ennui* (1809) can be seen to suggest that Scotland could be Ireland's future.[48] Again, the framework of the novel uses a young inheritor travelling in the hitherto unknown territory of Ireland, a device which allows a didactic demonstration of (often unsatisfactory) Irish mores. But the entire situation is subverted by the revelation that the inheritor actually began life as a local peasant lad, thanks to a long-ago exchange at birth. Over and above the nature-and-nurture implications lies the idea of improvement, and the archaism of the rebel intrigues swirling around the edges of the Irish world (once more, a prevision of *Waverley*). The idea that Ireland might follow Scotland's path under the Union was frequently advanced by the more optimistic contributors to the *Edinburgh Review* in the first thirty years of the nineteenth century. But the contrasts continued to be as pronounced as the parallels—not least in the untroubled way that Unionist, Anglicized, un-Gaelic Scots Lowlands culture used Highland tropes in constructing a Scottish identity within the Union. This was very different to the gingerly and sometimes agonized approach of the Anglo-Irish towards the potent Gaelic-Irish inheritance, which never lent itself to domestication in the manner of the Romantic myth of the Highlands. Certainly Irish eighteenth-century antiquarian historians had a shot at constructing a reassuringly commercial, bourgeois Milesian culture in the dim and distant past, but it remained a rather arcane fantasy, and brought no comfort for the present.[49] The Scots, unlike the Irish, contrived to have it both ways, from that day to this. And the reason Ireland did not become Scotland was closely linked to religious profession: a central issue to most writers of the nineteenth century, if not to some of their later critics.

III

The Irish novel, nonetheless, had achieved a head start by the 1820s, and reading the *Edinburgh Review* is a good way to realize this. What happened to it then? The 'national tale' fades out after the 1820s, as many critics have noted; this is because Catholic Emancipation in 1829 removed one of the major rationales and motive forces behind it. But would it be replaced by a fiction of everyday life? The novels of English realism are sometimes seen as a deliberate formalization of the values of settlement, stability, hierarchy, and social harmony—which are held to be irrelevant to the disruptions and antagonisms of Irish history and its—yet again—putatively 'unfinished' nature.[50] This theory is neat, but perhaps tends to the overdetermined and retrospective. It also means that when an Irish realist fiction does appear, it is sometimes written off as 'English' in its inspiration.[51] This may work for Trollope's Irish novels (though I have my doubts) but not for Irish practitioners such as John Banim, or Charles Lever, or William Carleton, or—eventually—Somerville and Ross. (Banim's *The Nowlans*, like the genre paintings of John Mulvany, in fact provides solid evidence of a comfortable Irish rural middle class at a time when literary theorists tend to deny that such a thing existed.) It might be added that the peculiarities

of Irish fiction may not always be specifically Irish peculiarities, as the renewed attention to Scottish novelists such as Hogg
and John Galt is beginning to demonstrate. The intention to
impose an 'improvement' ethos is apparent in Scott's fiction
much as in Edgeworth's, and the underlying theme of economics, Edinburgh-style, accompanies that of seductive, honourable
but outmoded Jacobitism.[52] It is hard nowadays to agree with
Georg Lukács's influential interpretation of Scott as somehow
operating in a vacuum created by his own protean energies, and
creating single-handedly the historical novel built around a historically representative character anchored in a thick description
of his times. Reading Scott's Irish contemporaries and anticipa-
tors is enough to give one second thoughts. But these writers—
Edgeworth, Owenson, Maturin—tend now to be pigeonholed
as the authors of 'national tales' (a popular subtitle from Owenson's debut onwards), while Scott is identified as the inventor
of the historical novel, to be imitated unsuccessfully in Ireland
by forgotten figures like the Banims, Gerald Griffin, and even,
bizarrely, Isaac Butt: the partial exception being John Banim's *The
Boyne Water* (1826), where the Scott formula is applied to Ireland
during the Williamite Wars, with strong echoes of *Old Mortality*.
Here, too, however, the 'national tale' convention introduces the
discordances of the present, as the broken Treaty of Limerick at
the end of the book clearly stands for the withholding of Catholic Emancipation at the time of writing. Nor does the subplot
of romance across the religious and ethnic divide end in a happy
resolution.[53]

In fact there are many early-nineteenth-century novels dealing with Irish history, featuring 1798 as well as 1690. It is more

FIGURE 10 John Banim

persuasive to see (as Katie Trumpener does) the national tale and the historical novel as stages of a linked development—with the two genres continuing an intertwined existence, in terms of borrowings and cross-fertilizations.[54] But how far the production of 'national tales' can be projected into the construction and development of nationalism per se is less certain. The fact that *Castle Rackrent* was neatly published in 1800, the year of the Union, has allowed an assumption that it initiated a process of fictional examinations of the Irish psyche, consciously connected to a new era in Anglo-Irish relations. But the process stretches back into the eighteenth century, and can be connected to the 'patriot' values of Grattanism rather than proto-nationalism. This syndrome continues. There is a particularly savage critique of British government of Ireland in Thomas Moore's satirical *Memoirs of Captain Rock, the Celebrated Irish Chieftain, with Some Account of His Ancestors, Written by Himself* (1824), a fiction which has echoes of *Castle Rackrent* but should certainly be seen as a national tale—'reshuffled', in Emer Nolan's suggestive phrase.[55] The convention of an 'old family' abused by history and retreating to a Gaelic fastness was by now well established in novels by Owenson, Maturin, and Edgeworth: Moore projects it satirically into the creation of an outlaw, whose self-exculpatory and unreliable narration carries echoes of King Corny as well as Thady Quirk. He also filters the text of the Captain's family history through an innocent English traveller, whose eyes are opened by degrees to the follies of bad British government—which is praised ironically by the Captain for thoughtfully catering to the Irish 'taste' for discord and insurrection. The history of the 'family', which for the first eleven hundred years of the Christian era is a record of achievement, is clearly that of the Irish nation. At the end of the book, though the Captain is transported to the hulks, the continuation of the family fortunes through violence and discord is ensured by the current government, which is sarcastically thanked for providing this service.

For some contemporary Irish radicals, Moore's satirical treatment seemed both lightweight and well worn, simply presenting 'the blasted heath; the craggy cliffs; poesy made tame; history run wild; the goblins and hobgoblins, hags, witches and tartan of Caledonia, dressed up in Pictish phase', to amuse the English.[56] But *Captain Rock* is an accomplished polemic on the state of the nation, the abuses of the Union, and the iniquity of withholding Catholic Emancipation. It is equally certain that by the time he wrote it, Moore was far from being a revolutionary nationalist, and that his chief venom was directed at those 'Parliamentary Judases' who had betrayed the Catholic cause.[57] When he writes in 1828 that 'my first inspiration shall be my last—the cause of

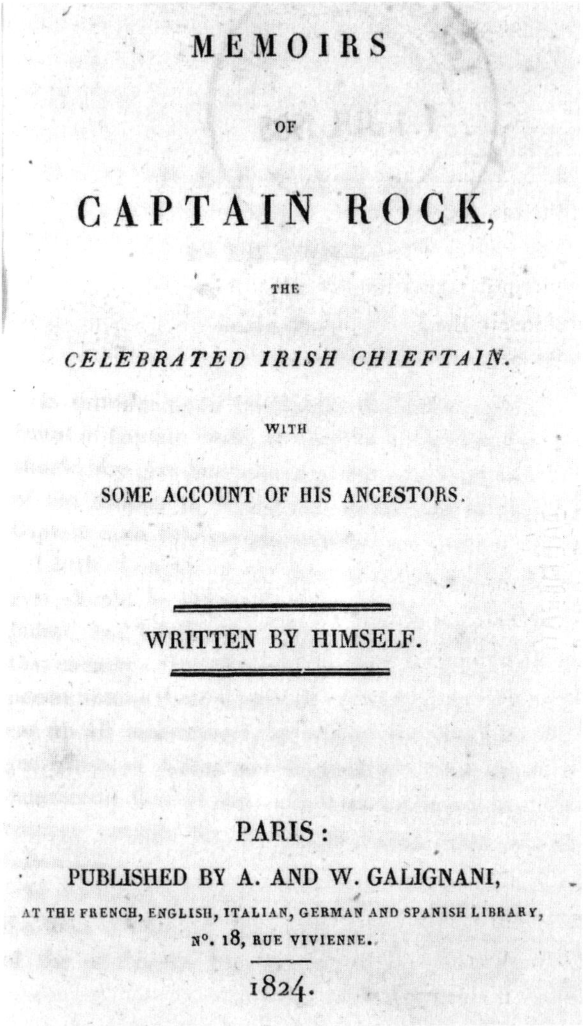

MEMOIRS

OF

CAPTAIN ROCK,

THE

CELEBRATED IRISH CHIEFTAIN.

WITH

SOME ACCOUNT OF HIS ANCESTORS.

WRITTEN BY HIMSELF.

PARIS:

PUBLISHED BY A. AND W. GALIGNANI,

AT THE FRENCH, ENGLISH, ITALIAN, GERMAN AND SPANISH LIBRARY,
Nº. 18, RUE VIVIENNE.

1824.

FIGURE 11 Title page of first edition of *Captain Rock,* 1824

Irish freedom' he is, just like Owenson, referring to emancipat-
ing his fellow Catholics from civil disabilities, not liberating the
Irish people from the English yoke. To see the early-nineteenth-
century national tale as 'setting out to address issues of Irishness'
and in the process raising the question of 'slavery' and 'defensive orientalism' may involve some over-interpretation. It is similarly risky to describe Owenson, on the strength of *The O'Briens
and the O'Flahertys*, as 'a pro-United Irish writer'.[58] Murrough
O'Brien, the attractive hero of that novel, becomes a United
Irishman in a moment of passion; but his 'good angel' cousin,
the beautiful Abbess who watches over his destiny and acts as
his *cicerone* through Roman intrigues and French Revolutionary politics as well as 1790s Dublin, clearly sees it as a mistake
from which he must be rescued. The fact that she also relishes
suggestive repartee as much as any Stendhalian *femme du monde*,
eventually renounces her vows, and marries Murrough (by that
stage a Napoleonic general) might remind us that Sydney Owenson's own politics are those of sceptical Irish Whiggery. This is
borne out by her correspondence and later writings. The 'issues
of Irishness' that concerned her were policies of improvement,
justice for Catholics, and reconciliation with an enlightened government, when one should arrive.

Nor does a serious engagement with the traditions of Gaelic
Ireland, common to all 'national tales', necessarily imply a politically nationalist agenda. Owenson, in a phrase misleadingly suggestive of modern literary criticism, describes Ireland as 'a text,
whose spirit and whose letter were mis-rule and oppression'.[59]
But she is writing in the 1820s, and the past tense should be
noted; this is not a manifesto for contemporary nationalism. The

plot of *The O'Briens and the O'Flahertys* cleverly brings together the remnants of Gaelic aristocratic society in the West of Ireland with the structures of polite Dublin society in the later years of Grattan's Parliament: Murrough, a Trinity student with French opinions, moves between the two, as—on a different level—does his father. Lord Arranmore, having begun his career as a clever apostate solicitor whose *converso* status is disapproved of by his Catholic relatives, ends it by ruining himself in pursuit of the revival of ancient family honours. His irresistibly handsome son, after undergoing sundry sexual temptations in Dublin viceregal circles, finds salvation of a sort by joining the new European order, and throughout the Continental identities and affiliations of the Gaelic tradition are heavily emphasized. But the novel ends with a heavy hint that the Napoleonic juggernaut is no more likely to provide deliverance for Ireland than a violent rebellion.

Owenson's political message sits almost as awkwardly with later nationalist rationalizations as the conservatism of Edgeworth or the anti-Catholic scare-politics of Maturin (played down by recent commentators). In fact, given the diversity and variety of authors peddling 'national tales', retrospectively decoding any overarching political pattern is rife with danger. Recent literary criticism has reinvigorated interest in these novels by imaginatively inserting them into the complex discourse of British identity-formation and imperial politics. This echoes and replicates what historians have been doing in another sphere.[60] Where the 'national tale' is concerned, this kind of critical re-examination also involves looking at the engagement with, and reinvention of, a traumatic history—again, echoing the preoccupation of recent historians discussing the same period. The retrospective idealization of the Grattanite period of the late eighteenth century is one common theme; so is the varying use of the memory of the 1641 rebellion, the Williamite Wars, and the 1798 Rising. But whether this makes the national tales of the early nineteenth century 'novels of insurgency', as one enthusiastic critic has called them, is another matter.[61]

The connection between 'national tale' and historical novel is certainly very close: closer, perhaps, than the connection to contemporary travel literature posited by some critics. To read these novels as a species of travel literature, conducting the reader across strange and barbarous terrain, presupposes that the intended audience is purely English, which may be an assumption too easily made. There was an Irish, Catholic, middle-class readership. Scott, again, visiting in 1825, was struck by this: he had been warned that publishing and book sales had fallen off in Ireland, thanks to the effects of the Union, but saw no sign of it. And a critical 'national tale' like John Banim's *The Anglo-Irish of the Nineteenth Century* (1828) seems to be addressed to an Irish audience at least as much as to an English one. The same is true of *The Boyne Water*, published two years earlier. The idea that Ireland is inevitably to be presented as 'strange', 'other', anomalous, peculiar or exotic to, and even by, the Irish themselves reminds us once more of Joep Leerssen's notion of 'auto-exoticism': a brilliant coinage at the time, which perhaps has had as much exposure as it deserves. It is certainly true that the early nineteenth century saw a powerful and partly realized impetus to amass statistical, economic, and sociological information about Ireland—all the more so as the problem of Irish poverty came to preoccupy Irish observers acutely, along with the question of whether Irish violence was endemic.[62] It is also undeniable that the early nineteenth century saw a great boom in the literature of the 'tour' of Ireland, as of other places. The connection between these phenomena and the emergence of the 'national tale' variety of Irish fiction, however, is more easily asserted than proven. And the random, disconnected, fragmentary nature of Irish 'tour' literature *may* indicate a significant incoherence, 'denying Ireland national wholeness and perpetuating stereotypes of incomprehensibility that reinforce an imperialist consciousness':[63] or it may just reflect the way that travel literature is cut and pasted together for a quick market sale, now as then.

Questions of over-interpretation recur. How far the fictions dubbed 'national tales' were specifically read as sociological or didactic treatises is debatable. Some contemporaries—including Irish contemporaries—certainly thought that this was an intended part of their function, and later critics certainly see a problematically England-directed vector influencing the authors' intended audience. This in turn reflects the fact that these are works written within the framework of a political union incorporating Ireland. Reconciliatory arrangements, at the end of an educational journey, provide the desired end: 'the Glorvina solution', in a shorthand referring to the marriage at the end of *The Wild Irish Girl*. Here, the hero Horatio reaches the end of his *bildungsroman* journey by a union with the woman who through harp-playing and history lessons has revealed Irish tradition to him, as the repository of a sophisticated, misunderstood culture. The marriage also solves a knotty question of past dispossession and present injustice by fusing together legal ownership of an Irish estate in the present with the historical claims of the past, represented by the bride's ancient family of Gaelic princes. (Owenson being Owenson, the marriage also involves a son wrenching his father's intended bride away from him at the altar and claiming her for himself, but the Oedipal implications of that may be let pass.)

There are Continental parallels to the genre of the reconciliatory marriage putting to rest a history of conquest—usually occurring in other small and contested nations (though *Ivanhoe* should be remembered too). Like John Banim in *The Boyne Water*, however, Owenson refused to allow this encouraging option in *The O'Briens and the O'Flahertys*, written two decades after *The Wild Irish Girl*. Later still, forty years after the first book's runaway success, Owenson wrote a notably conservative and Unionist introduction to a new edition of *The Wild Irish Girl*, where she referred to the way that her novel had united 'national grievances and historic fact'. That book, influential far beyond its literary merits, had set the tone both for polemicizing the Irish past and exoticizing the Irish present. Irish modes are presented as different, not inferior—and different because shaped by local needs and historical conditioning. Irish manners are presented as arising from defunct aristocratic modes, not from savage naivety. The aristocratic Irish native, Glorvina, is accomplished, sophisticated, intellectual: 'Wild' is a joke which did not make it into the many translations of the novel (the literal German title is 'The Nature-maiden', the French 'The Young Irishwoman'). The upper-class Irish Catholics in *The O'Briens and the O'Flahertys* slip constantly into French and Italian—an indication of their enforcedly peripatetic lives as well as their cultured educations. Edgeworth makes a similar point about the Continentalism of elite Catholic Irish manners in *Ormond*, and elsewhere. National tales usually involve the innocent hero learning a new cultural code, much as the hero of Edgeworth's *The Absentee* has to unlearn his mother's affected social language as the first step to becoming a reforming resident landlord. The theme of translation from Irish, very specifically addressed in *The Wild Irish Girl* in terms of song and music, stands for a wider dissonance of understanding, too—as it does in Thomas Moore's work. And it is central to Edgeworth's consciousness, notably in her *Essay on Irish Bulls*—though her manipulation of publicity and her positioning in the literary marketplace is instructively different to Owenson's or Moore's or John Banim's. They were necessarily more combative and more self-advertising—and, by the 1820s, more specifically bent on the redress of Catholic civil grievances.

By then, too (and here Michael and John Banim's historical novels *The Croppy* and *The Boyne Water* are important), the success of Scott dictated the form of the historical novel, set at a time of crisis but projecting forward to an era of improved promise.[64] The Banims' books (and those of others) rather query the assumption that Irish literary history was somehow marooned after the national tale had run its course and lurched into Gothic around the time of the Famine. Nonetheless one recent critic, ignoring the Gaelic background and Catholicism of the Banims, Griffin, and others, describes their fictions in terms of 'Anglican Ireland's need to usurp Ireland's native traditions to bolster its own public sphere';[65] Anglo-Irish novelists are therefore damned if they write about Gaelic Ireland, and damned if they don't. Other commentators have asserted that the English

realist tradition vampirizes the varied and energetic manifestations of fictional activity in its Celtic peripheries, while the
'national tale' moves from didactic attempts at providing sociological nostrums to 'critical sociologies of colonist society'. In
the process, celebratory nationalism and transcultural unions are
abandoned and rapprochement of various kinds becomes more
and more unlikely. This is arresting and suggestive, but may not
fit *Captain Rock* or *The Nowlans*.[66] The easy elision of 'national'
into 'nationalist' also raises problems when considering Moore
no less than Owenson. But it is undeniably true that fiction
immediately post-1800 often attempts to reconcile a celebration
of cultural distinctiveness with the possibilities of reconciliatory
union, while Irish novels of the late 1820s and beyond are more
complex and disillusioned.

Irish fiction post-Catholic Emancipation, such as Samuel Ferguson's *Hibernian Nights' Entertainments* or Carleton's *Traits and
Stories of the Irish Peasantry* and *Fardorougha the Miser*, bears this
out.[67] But the complexity of these fictions is not immediately
clarified by interpreting them in terms of 'settler' communities,
collaborator elites modelling their productions on an imperial
metropolis, or even as the result of a 'creole-type' colonial consciousness, as has recently been attempted. Fashionable as Third
World parallels are, it seems to me more profitable to consider
the Irish position in the early nineteenth century as resembling
Scotland's some time before; to consider in this light the entry of
Catholic intellectuals into the public sphere from the time of the
Union, gathering pace with Catholic Emancipation; to consider
the state of journalism and publishing in Dublin as in Edinburgh;
to consider the politics of O'Connellism, with all that implies for

public language, iconography, education, and religious identity; to consider the growth of nineteenth-century Irish fiction not only against the politics of the moment, but against the pre-history of eighteenth-century novel-writing, recently brought back into view. 'Book History', in the sense of publishing history, reception, reviewing, and the Darntonesque 'communications circuit', is easier to trace for early-nineteenth-century Edinburgh than for contemporary Dublin, largely because of the close attention paid to the pre-existing networks of the Enlightenment, and the rich sources of Edinburgh periodical publishing. But it is beginning to be possible. Recent treatments of Irish drama and Irish critical discourse in the early nineteenth century have emphasized the vitality and confidence demonstrated in other literary spheres besides fiction.[68] But in looking at the conditions of production of Irish literature, contemporary structures of education tend to be ignored and religion oversimplified—compared with Scotland.

Starting historically rather than theoretically, we might be able to interrogate more closely literary questions such as the absence of an Irish Walter Scott, the Irish alternatives to George Eliot, and the fact that the Irish Literary Revival of the late nineteenth century centred itself on poetry and drama rather than on fiction; it should be remembered nonetheless that much of Yeats's early work was made up of short stories and attempted novels. Looking at Irish readers and what has conditioned them (as J. R. R. Adams and Niall Ó Ciosáin have done) might confer a valuable perspective: for instance, Adams's careful demonstration that a taste for sensationalism was well established among the Irish reading public by the early nineteenth century is rarely

employed in analysis of Irish Gothic. The growth in sophistication of literary biography might also argue for immersion in the
lives of the writers themselves—Edgeworth's copious letters,
Owenson's memoirs, Moore's huge Journal—before rushing to
generalizations about the intentions behind their work.

Such an approach might make us consider rather carefully the
retrospective wishful thinking that characterizes a good deal of
politicized literary history, especially when sentimental recycled
Jacobitism discovers the language of psychoanalytical criticism.
When Walter Scott's use of the bardic past is described as 'the
alienized self depicting one's native landscape as a pornogra-
phized body for the stranger's gaze, a body which is composed
of absence of self as well as presence, which withdraws from
the gaze it evokes to preserve its humanity, its secret space, its
impenetrability', it is hard not to remember Scott's own warn-
ings about 'the mechanical jargon of French criticism'.[69] The way
that national inflections are being analysed in the literature of
Romanticism is an exciting development, but a historical dimension and context needs to be kept firmly in view; otherwise
the contributions of a highly politicized literary criticism may
obscure more than they clarify.[70] This is not new, particularly in
Irish literary criticism over the last century or so. Later commentators have been robustly sceptical about the claims for disinter-
ested political ecumenicism, and the sincerity of a progressive
agenda, periodically posited by nineteenth-century Irish novelists from a variety of backgrounds.[71] Hindsight suggests that this
programme was an impossibility in Ireland. But matters were
not so obviously cut and dried at the time, and it would be a
mistake to ignore contemporary mentalities by dismissing what

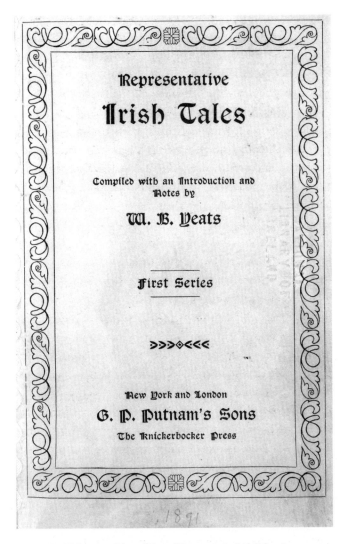

FIGURE 12 Title page of first edition of *Representative Irish Tales*, 1891

writers like Edgeworth, Owenson, Banim, and Moore thought they were doing; a great deal of valuable material worth analysing is preserved in their fictions and in the records of their lives.

This was noted by one ambitious critic at the end of the century, intent on defining the canon of Irish literature as well as transforming it by his own creative contribution. In 1891 the young W. B. Yeats, fresh from *The Wanderings of Oisin*, published the anthology *Representative Irish Tales*. Generally forgotten now, his choice is full of interest in its implications and its agenda: he spotted early on that the enterprise would also be 'a kind of social history'.[72] It starts with *Castle Rackrent* and is heavily weighted in favour of Carleton, the Banims, and Griffin. Yeats locates all these writers in close historical context, cutting his teeth as an impressive and original critic. Years later he remembered that 'during the first years of my literary life, I read [the Irish novelists] continually, seeking in them an image of Ireland that I might not forget what I meant to be the foundations of my art, trying always to winnow as I read... it was from the novelists and poets that I learned in part my symbols of expression.'[73] The rest of this book will prospect some of the traditions and inspirations he absorbed from his avatars. And it is worth remembering that Yeats also instructed the novelists and critics of his own day, when considering their early-nineteenth-century predecessors, to 'cast off a habit of mind which would compress a complex, incalculable, indecipherable nation into the mould of a theory'.[74] He was, as so often, wise in his generation.

2

The First Romantics: Young Irelands between Catholic Emancipation and the Famine

On 14 September 1845 Jane Welsh Carlyle wrote from Chelsea one of her flirtatious and sardonic letters—a thank-you for a gift of a book, *Ballad Poetry of Ireland*. The recipient was someone to whom she had 'sworn an everlasting friendship at first sight' and for whom she felt 'what my husband [Thomas] would call "a real, genuine healthy desire"' to see again. She continues:

> When *are* you purposing, thro the strength of Heaven, to break into open Rebellion? I have sometimes thought that in a Civil War I should possibly find my 'mission' *moi*! But in these merely *talking* times a poor woman knows not how to turn herself: especially if, like myself, she 'have a Devil'—always calling to her 'March! March,' and bursting into infernal laughter when requested to be so good as to specify, *whither*![1]

There are multiple ironies here. She was writing to Charles Gavan Duffy in Dublin, the young editor of the *Nation*, a phenomenally successful journal which since its foundation three

FIGURE 13 Jane Carlyle by Samuel
Laurence, 1848

years earlier had become the voice of Irish nationalism—first call-
ing for repeal of the Union and now, after the failure of Daniel
O'Connell's 'Repeal Year' of 1843, set on a more radical course.
Duffy would, through his newspaper, effectively call for armed
revolution in 1848 and be tried for treason. Others of his Young
Ireland group would be transported for their failed rising against
British rule. The era of experimental Unionism and a possible
via media for Ireland had disappeared, and, with it, hopes that
Ireland's development within the United Kingdom might resem-
ble Scotland's. The 'talking times' were clearly over.

Jane Welsh Carlyle's affectionate relations with potential Irish
rebels sound like the antithesis of all that her husband Thomas
Carlyle stood for. His sulphurous opinions of Irish immigrants,
in their 'rags and laughing savagery', had been published in his
treatise *Chartism* only six years before. 'The Irish National Character is degraded, disordered; till this recover itself nothing is yet
recovered. Immethodic, headlong, violent, mendacious: what

46

can you make of the wretched Irishman?...A people that knows not to speak the truth, and to act the truth.'[2] With Charles Kingsley, he has been consistently held up as an exemplar of the racist attitudes held by Victorian Britain towards the inhabitants of the sister island.[3] Yet his profuse letters to Duffy are as excited, affectionate, and teasing as his wife's; he kept in close contact with 'dear Duffy' up to the time of his death, visiting him in Dublin in 1846, writing in his defence when he was on trial, supporting him through his imprisonment, and—perhaps most surprisingly—initiating another visit to Ireland in 1849. They toured the country together when it was suffering the effects not only of a failed rebellion, but three years of catastrophic famine. Publishing his reminiscences of their friendship in 1892, Duffy wrote:

> I was engaged for nearly half the period...in the conflict of Irish politics, which from his published writings one might suppose to be utterly intolerable to him; but the readers of these letters will find him taking a keen interest in every honest attempt to raise Ireland from her misery, reading constantly, and having sent after him, wherever he went, the journal [i.e., the *Nation*] which embodied the most determined resistance to mis-government from Westminster, and throwing out friendly suggestions from time to time how the work, so far as he approved of it, might be more effectually done. This is the real Carlyle...[4]

This suggests a more complex picture; the huge series of Carlyle's published letters adds to it, and also demonstrates the immediate interest he took in the three 'real hot and live Irishmen' who were introduced to his drawing-room by Frederick Lucas in April 1845.[5] The young men were John Pigot, John

FIGURE 14 Thomas Carlyle
in 1845

O'Hagan, and Duffy himself. Both sides came away with their
prejudices shaken. Duffy believed that Carlyle knew 'next to
nothing, accurately or circumstantially, of Irish affairs' and could
be converted to being an advocate; Carlyle subsequently wrote to
him that 'Ireland, which means many millions of my own breth-
ren, has again a blessed chance in having made a man like you to
speak for her'.[6] (In the same letter he enlisted Duffy's help with
revisions to the Irish section of his life of Cromwell, willingly
given.) Mrs Carlyle, for her part, thought that the charismatic
Pigot could become the Robespierre of an Irish revolution (he
didn't; he became a very rich lawyer at the Indian Bar). This may
all seem ironic in retrospect, but ironies are part of the Young

FIGURE 15 Charles Gavan
Duffy

Ireland story: not the least being the post-revolutionary career of
Duffy himself.

More relevant to the 1840s and Irish Romantic nationalism is
the fact that, despite Carlyle's splenetic remarks about the Irish
poor in *Chartism*, Duffy and his Young Ireland friends saw themselves as the Chelsea prophet's 'sworn disciples' in philosophical
terms. The continuous connection of past and present, the eter-
nal spirit of the nation, the notion of heroic destiny, the effort to
saturate oneself in the atmosphere of history until the curtain
of the past could lift and allow through an illuminating beam,
the idea of History itself, in true Romantic style, as a progressive
regression—all these Carlylean themes can be tracked through
the ballads and historical reconstructions which the *Nation* pioneered from 1843.[7] They also came to agree with Carlyle that
Daniel O'Connell was a 'Prince of Humbug'. And above all

they were inspired by Carlyle's scorching attacks on Utilitarianism: 'Manchester' was the real enemy and moral regeneration the answer. The meeting in Carlyle's Chelsea house is in its way an epiphany in Irish cultural history, just as it was a formative moment in Duffy's life and the birth of an enduring friendship. It might also be seen as a key moment in the history of Irish Romanticism, though Carlyle's name rarely appears in nationalistic treatments of Irish literary history.[8]

The deputation of young nationalist intellectuals who visited Carlyle did not include two of the most influential writers in the Young Ireland group, John Mitchel and Thomas Davis. Mitchel, an Ulster Unitarian of violent opinions, was perhaps most powerfully affected by Carlyle, and much of his writing (as his editor Duffy complained) was heavily inflected by Carlylean stylistic tricks. The work of the more irenic and charismatic Davis, who provided most of the poetry and historical commentary for the *Nation* until his premature and sudden death in September 1845, is more easily related to contemporary Continental models of national-liberationist literature, though he seems to have imbibed them through reading rather than foreign travel. A Trinity College-educated Protestant (English father, Irish mother), he remains the symbolic figure of the movement, though Duffy has claims to being the moving spirit.

The culture of Young Ireland, as this group became called, would supply Irish nationalist writing with a powerfully mobilizing rhetoric for the next century. This revolved around historical set-piece reconstructions, an obsession with creating ballad and epic, invocations of swords, chains, tyrants, and martyrs, and a determination to educate the nation into consciousness of its

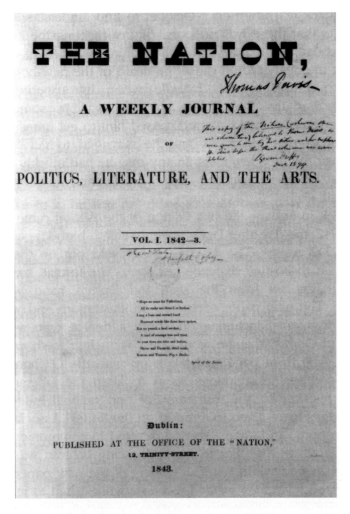

FIGURE 16 Thomas Davis's copy of the first issue of the *Nation*

own nationhood. This should be situated in the context of Irish life after Catholic Emancipation in 1829. Irish Romantic nationalism is too often seen retrospectively, looking back through the prism of the failed 1848 Rising—for all Jane Carlyle's ironic anticipations in 1845. The rhetoric of swords did take over from what she called the 'talking times' in the end. But it is doubtful if this would have happened without the advent of famine, the British government's spectacularly inadequate response in dealing with it, and—less obviously but very importantly to contemporaries—the expectations roused by events in Continental Europe. Young Irelands were born out of an Irish Romantic 'moment' going back to the 1830s, when other futures apparently opened up, and their pedigree can be traced through the intellectual life of Young Dublin as much as Young Ireland. This mobilization would be oddly repeated in Dublin half a century later, with the literary nationalism of revived 'Young Ireland Clubs' in the 1880s.[9] The precedents set by Davis and Duffy were closely noted by Yeats and his contemporaries, providing both political inspiration and aesthetic warning.

But the original Young Ireland itself owed something to precedent. An important influence behind it was the creation of another nationally minded journal in 1833, a decade before the *Nation*—the *Dublin University Magazine*. This organ reflected the opinions and talents of literary minded Protestant Tories such as Isaac Butt, Samuel Ferguson, and Sheridan Le Fanu. It was set up as a response to what seemed the inauguration of a new political dispensation, immediately following the era surveyed in the last chapter. Political reform, and a series of threats to the privileged position of the Anglican Church of Ireland and its members in

Irish life, had come in the wake of Catholic Emancipation in 1829. Thus far, thus defensive, and thus embattled. The splenetic Protestant fulminations emanating from the magazine under Butt's editorship from 1834 shocked his more liberal contributors like Ferguson. But the other cultural energies of Tory Ireland in this era have been neglected and to a certain extent misapprehended—as some striking recent work on Irish conservative politicians and writers such as John Wilson Croker, and Emerson Tennent has shown.[10] And the work of Joseph Spence established some time ago that the reactionary origins of the *DUM* coexisted with a pronounced appeal to 'national feeling', aimed specifically at disorientated Irish Protestants, and at times directed violently against the ignorant interference of English misgovernment. (An important early article was titled 'English Theories and Irish Facts', a recurring theme.[11]) This is the mentality that produced foundational texts such as Samuel Ferguson's 'Dialogue between the Head and Heart of an Irish Protestant', anticipating by some years the publication in the *Nation* of Thomas Davis's *Letters of a Protestant, on Repeal*. The political presuppositions may have been different, but the diagnosis of Irish Protestant mentality post-Emancipation is curiously similar.

Moreover, the key writers William Carleton and James Clarence Mangan occupied an interstitial space between the two journals, writing for both and linked to the editorial cabals in both. Nor are the politics of the *DUM* always as Orange as might be expected. It shared with the *Nation* a cult of the late eighteenth century in Ireland and Grattan's Parliament; and allowed that Repeal was 'a senseless but not uncaptivating cry'.[12] The articles which it published, like those in the *Nation*, highlighted

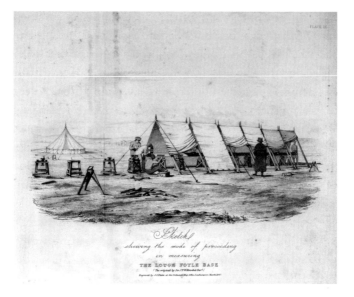

FIGURE 17 The Ordnance Survey conducting measurements at Lough Foyle, 1827

place-names, authenticity, the reclamation of saga and epic literature, fairylore, and the exploration of Ireland's topography. This
was also the era of the Irish Ordnance Survey, which employed
the principal antiquarian scholars of the time (Eugene O'Curry,
John O'Donovan, George Petrie) as researchers, along with the
poète maudit Mangan, albeit in a less exalted capacity.

The Ordnance Survey has come under examination recently,
denounced in some quarters as a blatant attempt to inscribe
colonial priorities on an abused landscape, and accused of insti-
tuting an 'Irish class system in miniature', with lowly Catholics
patronized by Ascendancy grandees.[13] This latter claim does not

seem substantiated by the correspondence between Ferguson and O'Donovan, or borne out by the *couche sociale* occupied by someone like George Petrie. What the Survey was trying to do, in its original ambitious scope (not long sustained), was to make an impressive attempt at historical reclamation, the rediscovery of local tradition, and the derivation of place-names: reading the landscape as a palimpsest layered with the experience of ancient invasions. Thus far, it may indeed have set a few alarm bells ringing in official minds. It certainly echoed much of the rhetoric of the *Nation*, which added a top-dressing composed of the hallowed deaths of heroes and the cult of sublime scenery.

This is most easily identified as Irish Romanticism, though Thomas Davis's most recent hagiographer bristles at the

THOMAS O. DAVIS
Poet and Politician
b.1814 ; d.1845.

Drawn from memory by Sir Frederick W. Burton, R.H.A. (1816-1900)
Presented by the Artist.

FIGURE 18 Thomas Davis by Frederic William Burton

description.[14] Young Ireland were Tocquevillian democrats too (the *Nation* constantly cites Gustave de Beaumont's 1839 commentary on Ireland's situation under British rule, based on a tour made in the company of de Tocqueville and much influenced by him[15]). However, the anti-materialist aspect of their thought is derived from Carlyle as much as from Burke and Grattan; and from Carlyle, too, comes their belief in a knowledge of history as the key to liberation. 'Its first political effect would be enormous; it would be read by every class and side...it would clear up the grounds of our quarrels, and prepare reconciliation; it would *unconsciously* make us recognize the causes of our weakness; it would give us great examples of men and of events, and materially influence our destiny.'[16] This manifesto was published in the same month as the editors' meeting with Carlyle.

The language of the nationally conscious Irish intelligentsia, on both sides of the political divide, is essentially what might be expected from the post-Walter Scott generation, even though the anticipated outpouring of *Waverley*-style novels with Irish themes did not appear.[17] But after the upheavals of the late 1820s and early 1830s the literary form which Irish Romanticism took among nationalist writers is dominated by Davis's synthetic ballads for the *Nation*, often quarried from the conflicts of Irish history and ending with stirring invocations to the present generation not to betray their forefathers through slavish quiescence. Since Davis was descended from Cromwellian planters on his mother's side, this had to be rather inconsistently blended with the rhetoric of religious pluralism and a recurring argument that Irish nationality needed the foreign strains imported over centuries of invasion, so long as their commitment was to the land of

Ireland. Invented history and Ossianic kitsch persisted: the search for authenticity may be illustrated by discoveries that appeared in the *Nation* such as 'The Voice of Tara—Date Unknown'.

> O! that my voice could waken the hearts that slumber cold! –
> The chiefs that time hath taken, the warrior kings of old! –
> Oh! For Fingal, the pride of all the gallant Fenian crew,
> To wave his brand—the fight demand—and blow the Baraboo!'

The editor added a helpful footnote.

> The original Irish of this song has been preserved in the extensive mountain tract that stretches far into the adjacent counties of Limerick, Cork and Kerry, between the towns of Newcastle, Abbeyfeale and Castleisland. I have vainly attempted to learn the author's name, but the original bears strong marks of its being the production of a Munster bard in the seventeenth century. I took it down, viva voce, from a Bacchach [cripple], who moved a very respectable repertory of wool, butter and antiquarian lore among the simple dwellers of the glens. He sung it to that very warlike air, vulgarly named 'The Poacher', in a kind of recitative, with his eyes closed, as if to shut out exterior objects from his inspired vision, and leaning on the top of his staff, as he swayed his body to and fro to the martial sounds. I have rendered the words as literally as possible, hopeless of preserving the abrupt and striking spirit of the Gaelic.[18]

Irish Romanticism, like Irish nationalism in general, does not fit neatly with a general world model; it retains its special variations. Unexpectedly, Romanticism in Ireland, for all its Gothic trimmings, was not inevitably Catholic. After Emancipation, and with the Anglican Church of Ireland threatened, the Romantic aesthetic—in church architecture as in literature—allowed local Protestants an opportunity to be 'national'.[19] This was exploited by the Young Turks of the *DUM*, no matter how Orange-tinted their backgrounds and politics, and the *Nation* delightedly proclaimed the fact.

> Twelve months ago, all the world could not produce a People so ignorant of their own history. To-day every man is familiar with it, or longs to be so. Its castles, its raths, its battle-fields have become classic and sacred ground. Its triumphs are sung in racy melodies in every cottage, farmhouse and mansion through the land, and in many a drawing-room. The young Conservative, hot with the fire of youth and the instinctive love of country, takes its history to his heart, and in his bigoted College he sighs in secret to 'strike a blow for his country'.[20]

This expressed a good deal of wishful thinking. Nonetheless the young Ulster Protestant lawyer Samuel Ferguson ransacked Irish history for his series of tales, *The Hibernian Nights' Entertainments* (1833–6), which borrowed a serial narrative device from celebrated Oriental precedents in order to exoticize the Irish past. His putative nationalism is less easily deduced from the literary controversy which began his career as a translator, when he pulled rank on James Hardiman's aggressively nationalist translations of early Gaelic poetry in his influential *Irish Minstrelsy*. Hardiman's interpretation of these poems as allegories against foreign oppression was brutally mocked by Ferguson, who assaulted it in a famously bruising review and substituted his own versions— undeniably superior if also implicitly political. He was, in fact,

FIGURE 19 Samuel Ferguson
by Frederic William Burton,
1848

determined to remove the *œuvre* from the Jacobite context which
Hardiman had stressed, and into which recent commentators
have reinserted them in our own day.

This suggests that Herder's idea of a lost bond between
genuine folk poetry and the spirit of a people might have to
be adapted for the purposes of Ireland's divided communities.
Both the nationalists of the *Nation* and the nationally conscious
Tories of the *Dublin University Magazine* believed (with Schlegel
and Carlyle) that the historian was a prophet facing backwards.[21]
But for Ferguson's purposes ancient Irish literature should be
identified with 'the old romantic life of the Irish nobleman'.
For all the violence of that vanished society, the world of the
bards and chieftains represented a time before the qualities of

patriarchalism and hierarchy had been perverted and exploited by the priesthood of Rome.[22]

Half a century later Standish O'Grady (another Young Carlylean) would preach a similar message—to the young Yeats among others.[23] Like O'Grady after him, Ferguson could combine Unionist politics with an endorsement of the original 'honourable' rebel heroes of the safely long-ago battles of Benburb and Aughrim. And in the 1830s he believed that a history of antagonism could usher in amity between present-day Catholics and Protestants. Addressing a personified Ireland, he asks:

> What though in times long past they startled your midnight echoes with our groans under the knife that spared neither bedridden age nor cradled infancy ... What though in sacred vengeance of that brave villainy we fattened two generations of your kites with the heads of traitors ... It was for love of you that we contested ... and now that the nuptial knot [of Union presumably] is tied and consecrated between us, nothing save the sword of Alexander shall dissolve that Gordian consummation.[24]

It is hard not to hear an assonance with Thomas Davis's national ballad 'Celt and Saxon':

> What matter that at different shrines
> We pray unto one God –
> What matter that at different times
> Our fathers won this sod –
> In fortune and in name we're bound
> By stronger links than steel;
> And neither can be safe nor sound
> But in the other's weal.[25]

FIGURE 20 Isaac Butt by John
Butler Yeats, 1876

Ferguson's editor Isaac Butt, equally productive, was simultaneously working as a barrister and delivering economic lectures as
a precocious Whately Professor at Trinity.

He, too, wrote fiction, culminating in a historical novel, *The
Gap of Barnesmore*, which appeared in 1848. He was not the only
Irish Tory of his generation to write admonitory novels which
show *Waverley* roots, involving Jacobite wars, kings in conflict,
feuding families, deranged native prophetesses, and heroines
whose suitors conveniently reflect different strains in Irish history.[26] But the Irish Tory writers show a subtle understanding of
Ulster, and a belief in the capacity of that peculiar province to
herald change in Ireland. Duffy would later confirm that Butt's
fiction, like Le Fanu's, was written with the conscious aim of
extending the spirit of nationality,[27] and these early inventions
have a particular interest, in the light of Butt's later career as

the instigator of the Home Rule project. In 1840 he published an uneven, eccentric but absorbing fiction called *Irish Life: In the Castle, the Courts, and the Country*, which shows Dublin as a ruin of Empire, loudly echoing Volney's quintessential Romantic imagery and providing some clues towards its author's future odyssey. Twelve years previously, in 1828, the O'Connellite John Banim had produced an equally uneven fiction called *The Anglo-Irish of the Nineteenth Century*. Edgeworthian in form, it traced the education of a young inheritor, who moved away from the notion that Ireland's salvation lay in adopting Anglicized modes, and towards an acceptance of national self-reliance: a stance anticipated by 'improvement' novels of an earlier era, notably *Maurice and Berghetta; or, The Priest of Rahery*, published in 1819 by none other than William Parnell, the grandfather of Butt's eventual successor as Home Rule leader.

Close assonances may be traced between Banim's 1828 work and Butt's *Irish Life*. Butt, too, brings a narrator from England, to examine Ireland's pretensions to nationality, the decadence of Dublin, and the necessity for moral rebirth (Emerson and Carlyle again); Orangeism is looked on critically, and the noble nationalist protagonist, O'Donnell, calls for a non-sectarian Ireland on a distinctly proto-Davisite model. The radical analogy is drawn of Venice groaning under the Austrian yoke—a stock-in-trade of *Nation* allegory.[28] And it was Butt also who, as early as 1837, laid out a manifesto for intellectual revival under the title 'The Past and Present State of Irish Literature'. Here the young barrister and economist showed the range of his preoccupations (and ambition) by discussing the reputation, appeal, and commercial potential of Irish writers in the English market, and the need to establish Dublin as a viable literary metropolis, with its own publishing industry. Again, one can find many answering echoes from the opposing side.[29] The *DUM* was—as the *Nation* would later be—preoccupied by the definition of Irish history as biography, beginning a 'Gallery of Illustrious Irishmen' series in 1836, which presented Irish identity as forged and expressed through Irish writing. Goldsmith was claimed as the first exemplar.[30] The *DUM* used the series to assert and define 'national principles' as pioneered by Swift and Berkeley: principles that were later, in its view, 'perverted' by O'Connell but still not past redemption. The central Carlylean idea of the individual life as vehicle and example of the larger history recurs.

Irish Romanticism delivered a visual punch, too, notably in George Petrie's landscapes and his depiction of pious pilgrims visiting scenes of antiquity. The messages behind the Cork painter Daniel Maclise's supercharged paintings of historical themes are more complex; recent scholarship firmly identifies him with the manufacture of English rather than Irish nationalism, as illustrated by his creation of 'Merrie England' images and his murals for the House of Lords, not to mention the Tory company he kept in the Maginn circle around *Fraser's Magazine*.[31] But his endlessly influential engravings illustrating Moore's melodies, and the message read (however inaccurately) from his bravura treatment of the Norman invasion in *The Marriage of Strongbow and Aoife*, gave concrete form to the images popularized in the *Nation*. Broken-stringed harps, languishing maidens, deposed chieftains were posed against a tragic landscape of ruined churches and sublime mountains. The poems that accompanied these pictures in the sensationally successful *Melodies* are returning to critical

FIGURE 21 Daniel Maclise, *The Marriage of the Princess Aoife of Leinster with Richard de Clare, Earl of Pembroke (Strongbow)*, 1854

vogue. Unlike his illustrator, Tom Moore's British political connections were all Whigs or radicals, but his and Maclise's trajectories echo each other. Both pursued stellar careers in early nineteenth-century London, closely integrated into metropolitan society, while they mined the lode of Irish history to create enduring Romantic and Romanticist images.

Maclise's imagination is saturated in Scott's chivalric and Romantic imagery, but he melds it with Irish historical visions in order to create, as Tom Dunne has said, a kind of history-painting that is dually British and Irish.[32] Moore's duality is of a different order. He is, after a period of neglect, coming into his own, with a number of recent studies, an excellent and sympathetic biography, new editions, and several works in the pipeline. Once he was seen by 'advanced nationalists' (including Yeats) as

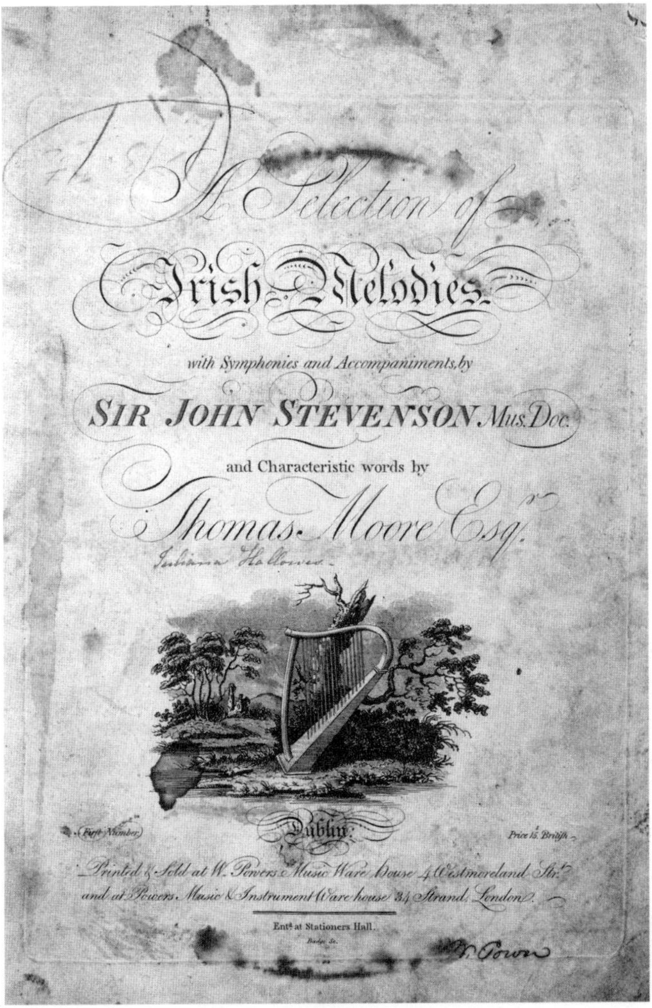

FIGURE 22 Thomas Moore's *Irish Melodies*, first number, 1808

a collaborator who turned his talent into sentimental drawing-room performances for the English elite. Nowadays his influence is recognized in constructing specifically Irish forms of poetic scansion and rhythm, projected forward through Ferguson and J. J. Callanan to Yeats.[33] Currently the political polemic invested in *Captain Rock* and *Lallah Rookh* (an Orientalist allegory of the state and Irish Catholicism) is the subject of much attention. Moore's own defence, that he intended to export the message of Irish historical wrongs into the courts of power, is given more due than used to be the case.[34] Recent analysis has also stressed his use of a particularly Irish blend of music and song and noted Moore's observation that Irish musical modes themselves reflect national character: his Romantic lyrics expressed traditional Gaelic fatalism and nostalgia as much as fashionable yearning.[35] The tropes of slavery, lost kingship. foreign tyranny, and present degradation, though usually intended to represent the cause of Catholic rights rather than national independence, anticipate the language of the *Nation* very closely. And though by the time of its first issue in October 1842 Moore's reputation was in decline and he was seen as lost to his native land, it is striking that he was chosen as the first person to be featured in the new paper's series 'Notable Irishmen'. The article begins defensively with an imagined critique: ' "Why in the devil's name did you put the little Whig into THE NATION at all?" "Because he is an Irishman, of whose genius Ireland is proud, and for whose services she is grateful." ' The article argued that having been overpraised he was now underestimated, heaped plaudits on works like *Captain Rock* and *The Life and Death of Lord Edward Fitzgerald*, provided a ringing defence of the drawing-room minstrel as an authentic patriot poet, and ended with a frank admission: 'We did not think we had much to say about Moore when we sat down—[but now] we know not how to stop writing about him.'[36]

In apostrophizing Tom Moore, Duffy and Davis were implicitly acknowledging that the *Nation* did not spring out of a vacuum. The heyday of Moore's generation, which included Owenson, Edgeworth, and Maturin, had passed, the first two retiring to England and the third burning out; Banim was dead and Griffin silenced. But a significant legacy had been left behind. For all Isaac Butt's dramatic imagination, the notion of Dublin thirty years after the Union as a Volney-esque ruin, like Rider Haggard's 'Mysterious Kôr', should not be given too much credence. The Irish publishing business continued to wax and wane but was far livelier than usually allowed; Rolf Loeber and Magda Stouthamer-Loeber have established a flourishing period for native Irish fiction in the 1820s and 1830s, confirmed at the time by William Carleton in the preface to his groundbreaking (if strictly unromantic) *Traits and Stories of the Irish Peasantry*.[37] It is generally accepted that publishing in Dublin was much inhibited by the operation of British copyright law after the Union, and the novelists mentioned in the last chapter invariably published their works first in London. However, writing in 1842, Carleton believed it was no longer the case that Irish *littérateurs* had to follow the example of landlords and become absentees. The Famine would darken this false dawn, but nonetheless some key figures continued to sustain Irish publishing—notably James Duffy, who enabled the production of the 'Library of Ireland' volumes inspired by his namesake at the *Nation*, as well as the bestselling volume of Davis's poems.[38]

The Library of Ireland appeared from 1844, in the form of shilling volumes of biography, poetry, and criticism; they amounted to a series of influential primers on Irish history, locally published and reaching many editions. The immediate proximity of Dublin's literary and political institutions in these decades is striking: the line from James Duffy's premises at Wellington Quay (and later Anglesea Street), to the *Nation*'s offices on D'Olier Street, to the forum for O'Connell's meetings in the Corn Exchange at Burgh Quay, to Trinity College and the *DUM*, makes a very tight triangle indeed. It might be extended to George Petrie's house in Great Charles Street, where the scholars of the Ordnance Survey met and worked—including figures like James Clarence Mangan

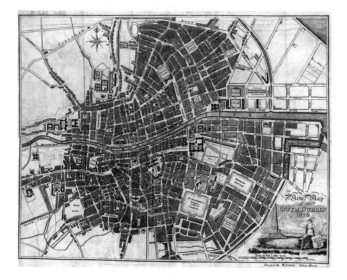

FIGURE 23 Dublin in 1829

in his dark-green eyeglasses, conical hat, and cloak, making his way between the various compass points in an opium haze.[39] Other habitués such as Charles Lever, future editor of the *DUM* and targeted venomously as an 'Irish Cockney' by the *Nation*, described a larger arc. It was not an all-male world: woman poets such as Jane Francesca Elgee ('Speranza') and Mary Anne Kelly ('Eva') were important influences in raising the revolutionary tempo of the *Nation*. Elgee provides another intersectional example between the worlds of the *Nation* and the *DUM*, though her contributions to the latter ended after she was found in the office in compromising circumstances with the editor Isaac Butt. Later she would marry Sir William Wilde and become vicariously famous all over again as the mother of Oscar.

Literary love-affairs remain obscure (it was Ireland, after all) but literary feuds were part of the landscape and so were literary friendships. For both, Charles Gavan Duffy's copious autobiographical writings are still the best guide.[40] The tendency to describe Ireland as a devastated cultural landscape between the Union and the literary renaissance of the 1890s needs to be countered; the distinct civic cultures of Dublin and Belfast in the pre-Famine era should be given their due. Samuel Ferguson, who had cut his literary teeth on *Blackwood's*, continued to live in hopes that Dublin might become 'a better Edinburgh'.[41] Belfast in the 1830s had Charles Teeling's pathbreaking *Ulster Magazine*, where Ferguson was first published, as well as the Belfast Literary Society, the Linen Hall Library, the Academical Institution, and other establishments owing much to the Scottish Enlightenment.

In many ways Ferguson, as Eve Patten has shown, was a personification of that ancient and creative connection across the narrow straits; though some critics prefer to see him as an imperialist imposing a proto-Arnoldian version of racialized Celticism and primitivity on his fellow Irishmen, this seems rather ahistorical. Plotting the cultural atmospherics of the 1830s and early 1840s in Ireland, reading the magazines of the era, and tracing the lives of the participants suggests more vividly the dynamics of collaboration through historical reclamation, affecting the intelligentsia across a wide range of endeavour. Romantic antiquarianism was hardly unusual in the era, and in Ireland it was necessarily adapted for special uses. But it is not often enough noted how the opposing traditions in Ireland after Catholic Emancipation attempted to stake out a common ground; as Thomas Davis put it to his friend Ferguson in 1845, shortly before his own premature death, 'There is something in our feelings about this country that makes us brothers.'[42] It should be no surprise that a dominant note of the *Nation*, when one reads through it from its origins in 1842, is the need to form common cause with Irish Protestants. Time and again Duffy's editorials and Davis's ballads (signed, inaccurately, 'A True Celt') stress this theme. It is compatible with profuse articles on ancient literature, and evaluations of contemporary Irish writers on the basis of their 'claims to national respect' (by the *Nation*'s criteria, Moore qualified triumphantly here, while Lever failed). This is accompanied by voluminous coverage of the doings of the Repeal movement, with blow-by-blow accounts of episodes such as the famous debate in Dublin Corporation between O'Connell and Butt.[43] But the *Nation* was also careful to cover court news and the doings of haut-bourgeois Dublin—and to highlight the loyal toasts to the Queen raised at Repeal dinners, after speeches excoriating 'slavery' and 'tyrants'.[44]

This inconsistency remained. The tone of the *Nation's* news coverage, its pluralistic editorial articles, and Davis's profuse *Letters of a Protestant, on Repeal* (fourteen of them by June 1843, reduced to five for publication) sit uneasily with the rhetoric of the same writer's ballads. But poetry was an essential vehicle. Davis's mentor, friend, and first editor, the Trinity don Thomas Wallis, recorded that

> all the founders of the *Nation* agreed in the resolve that, come whence it would, poetry—real living poetry, gushing warm from the heart, and not mechanically mimicking obsolete and ungenial forms—was worth a trial, as a fosterer of National feeling, and an excitement to National hope. But it came not from any outward source; and thereupon Davis and his companions resolved, in default of other aid, to write the poetry themselves. They did so; they surprised themselves and everybody else.[45]

This recalls Wesley's advice that in order to be endowed with predestined grace, it helped to pray that it might be so, and then you might find out that in fact you had it all along; or perhaps Mrs W. B. Yeats desperately taking up automatic writing to save her marriage and finding that it did the trick. There is certainly a sense of being put in touch with Unknown Instructors operating from a Jungian great unconscious. The messages coming through harp intensely on violence in the past, and its potential necessity in the future.[46] But the method by which national ballads came to Davis out of the vasty deep meant that, in a sense, he was not responsible for what they said; the poems he published under names like 'Celt' in the *Nation* were not, so to speak, his own. They belonged to 'the Nation' in more ways than one.

Thus Davis could engage in a kind of cultural politics that prefigures Yeats's enterprise a half-century later. National pride must be inculcated in a national literature. But, as Yeats would find, if the rediscovered national literature was to be read by influential people, it would necessarily have to be expressed in the language of the oppressor. This raised awkward questions and required some fancy footwork. Like the Ordnance Survey, which tried to find authentic but comprehensible versions of place-names, Davis preached linguistic reclamation. In order to 'efface the very footsteps of the foreign spoilator from our soil', he felt that agreed Gaelicist terms should be restored 'in the mouths of the people'. This campaign was robustly ridiculed by most of his colleagues on the *Nation*, who saw no point in referring to the River Shannon as the 'Sionnain'; some of them even expressed a subversive wish 'to be cosmopolitan and deviate occasionally from our native bogs'.[47] Language, like religion, was always going to be a sticky wicket; all the more need, then, to fall back on a cult of militarism and martyrdom as the necessary next step from literary consciousness-raising.

> The tribune's tongue and poet's pen
> May sow the seed in prostrate men;
> But 'tis the soldier's sword alone
> Can reap the crop so bravely sown![48]

International examples were often adduced, from Algeria, Greece, Poland, Italy, Bohemia, Serbia, and Hungary, while

William Tell made regular saintly appearances. The contradiction between denouncing the historical 'Saxon' and his incursions into Ireland, while holding out the hand of friendship to the Saxon's descendants in the country, was never completely resolved.[49] The right to bear arms and the idea of a civic militia represented preoccupations from eighteenth-century Ireland brought up to speed for current times, but the potential for creating civil instability would have been starkly clear to the government in the age of the Chartists. Daniel Maddyn pointed out the anomaly at the time: '[Young Ireland] professes principles which cannot be realized without resorting to a bloody civil war. Its songs, its vehement effusions, its ballads, may *disturb* society and ferment angry passions, but assuredly they can achieve nothing further than bestowing a literature

FIGURE 24 John Mitchel

on the popular passions of the Irish lower nation.'[50] Which was, in its way, a considerable ambition.

Several of the *Nation* team came from Ulster, and another theme traceable to their idealized memory of the eighteenth century was a marked penchant for Irish Presbyterians. A series of encouraging editorials approvingly reminded them of their fine record in the 1798 Rising. Presbyterians were attractive to the ideologues on the *Nation* not only because of their revolutionary past, but also because of their present alienation from the power structures of the Unionist elite, and their radical potential in terms of land agitation in Ulster. It is likely that this represented Duffy's interest, and to a certain extent Mitchel's; Davis's eighteenth-century obsession concentrated upon the perfect Protestant rebel Wolfe Tone, whose biography he intended to write. This interest is reflected in a series of long and historiographically useful articles recording the memories and testimony of Tone's widow, Matilda.[51] Tone's celebrated appeal to the 'men of no property' also struck a chord, for the *Nation* increasingly adopted the radical-democratic language of contemporary left-wing journals in Britain. 'Aristocracy' was condemned, as it applied to politics in Britain as well as landholding in Ireland (tenant right would remain a cause close to Duffy's heart, raising further Carlylean echoes). Chartist activity was fully and sympathetically covered. All this encouraged a powerful rhetoric of expectation, initially brought to fever pitch through 1843, which O'Connell declared would be 'Repeal Year'. When after a year of frenzied campaigning the Repealers backed down rather than defy the government's ban on a final huge demonstration, the *Nation* put a brave face on it, but it signalled

a shift. The newspaper continued to talk up the coming of independence, but it more and more looked to European parallels
and made analogies with European tyrannies. Notably, a cult of
Italy developed, with Ireland as 'the Italy of the West', England
playing Austria's villainous role, and France as a possible deliverer for both.[52] Davis's task up to his premature death in 1845 was
to nurture the expectation of apotheosis. He did not live to see
the two great annunciations which fixed Young Ireland's fate:
first the Irish Famine, and then the revolutions in Europe.

The arrival of the potato famine in 1846 put into sharp focus
the insufficiency of Britain's government of Ireland under the
Union. It also changed Irish literary consciousness, as has been
indicated in highly suggestive studies by Melissa Fegan and Christopher Morash.[53] Mangan's late poetry is now convincingly read
through this prism, and the conditions of the Famine inflect much
of the work of Carleton and other fiction writers in the starving
Forties. As the horror of the Famine spread, the *Nation*'s editorial
line was strangely uncertain. In part, the Famine was seen as a
punishment from God: 'a scourge of heaven for national sin', the
sin of dependence on a foreign power. 'They shall crawl and pine,
and whine and beg, and beg in vain, until they learn the worth
of a man's manhood—the infinite value and virtue of a nation's
independence!'[54] The journal also, for some time, rather huffily
repudiated the thought of accepting English charity. But as the
crisis escalated and the government response was seen more and
more clearly as inadequate to the point of malign neglect, the
effect on Irish domestic politics, and on politically minded intellectuals, became decisive. On the Tory side, it propelled Samuel Ferguson (temporarily) and Isaac Butt (eventually) in the direction of

repealing the Union. The issues of poverty and economic policy had preoccupied the *DUM* writers since the magazine's inception; Isaac Butt's Trinity lectures stated that the essential economic question was society's actual, versus its pretended, attitude to poverty, and at the end of the Famine Ferguson returned to the theme in a quizzical dialogue called 'Inheritor and Economist'.[55] Thus far, the early pluralist expectations of Young Ireland, and their hopes for national convergence, seemed to be borne out— precipitated by a subsistence crisis which queried in the starkest terms the logic of Union.

Young Ireland had already split from O'Connell in 1846 on the question of religious control of education in Ireland; O'Connell's subsequent death and his replacement by his son John made the breach impassable. By 1848 the desperate state of the country propelled Ferguson into the kind of initiative so long forecast by the *Nation*: a Protestant Repeal organization. Unsurprisingly, its every meeting received glowing coverage by Duffy. For a moment, Davis seemed not to have died in vain. Duffy himself had been influential in the conversion, publishing ten of Ferguson's poems in his edition of *Ballad Poetry of Ireland* (the book he gave to Jane Carlyle). This volume took Burns, on whom Ferguson had written, as one of its great exemplars of a national poet, and Ferguson produced some Ulster Scots verse which is pure Burns in its inspiration and presentation.[56] In many ways Ferguson, despite his savage attack on Hardiman ten years before, must have seemed ripe for the plucking. He had been friendly with Davis, and from 1845 became close to Thomas D'Arcy McGee and even Mitchel: the new wave of Young Irelanders, regrouping themselves into the more openly radical 'Irish Confederation'. The fact that the *Nation* gang had separated from O'Connell made them seem all the more attractive to someone of Ferguson's bent; transcendentalist moral regeneration, in the style of Carlyle and Mazzini, seemed to be replacing Catholic nationalism. Davis's death had inspired Ferguson's masterpiece, a 'Lament' for his friend cast in a deliberately Gaelic form and first published in the *DUM* with a memoir of the dead patriot, as an instalment of 'Our Portrait Gallery'. This was perhaps the closest interaction between the two journals.

And a year later Ferguson and some like-minded Protestants, driven beyond endurance by the failure of the British government to respond effectively to national starvation, came out as Protestant Repealers. Their arguments strikingly anticipate the early Home Rule movement twenty years later. They take up Butt's economic ideas in opposing the Poor Law's operations, and denounce Whig governments for imposing centralized policies irrelevant to Irish conditions. There was a sense that, if a British government rode roughshod over the interests of local Irish Protestants, they might do better to make their own terms with their Catholic fellow countrymen. The intriguing question must remain whether, without the Rising of 1848, this rapprochement would have gone further, anticipating the Home Rule demand by a generation, and keeping Protestant Ireland on board as part of the enterprise.

The first Protestant Repeal meeting was in May 1848, elaborately recorded in the *Nation*.[57] But another kind of radicalization was happening, too, chillingly foretold by Mangan in his highly characteristic 'New Year's Lay' featured in the *Nation* of

1 January 1848. Sardonically titled 'A Voice of Encouragement', it ended:

> Omen-full, arched with gloom, and laden with many a presage
> Many a portent of woe, looms the Impending Era.
> Not, as of old, by Comet-sword, Gorgon, or ghastly Chimera,
> Scarcely by Lightning and Thunder, Heaven today sends its message
> Into the secret heart—down through the caves of the spirit,
> Pierces the silent Shaft—sinks the invisible Token –
> Cloaked in the Hall the Envoy stands, his mission unspoken,
> While the pale banquetless guests await in trembling to hear it.

As people starved or died of famine fever in the face of government inaction, the rhetoric of expectation created by Duffy and Davis was adapted by John Mitchel, Thomas Francis Meagher, and others into something more specifically revolutionary—and republican. Their demand went beyond devolution: a republican national assembly on the Continental model rather than 'a golden link, or a patchwork parliament, or a College-Green chapel of ease to St Stephen's'.[58] For years the *Nation* had carried articles on French sympathies for Ireland (again, promulgating the cult of 1798). With the 1848 Revolution in France, placing the poet Lamartine in power, the auguries for Ireland seemed proven. Better still, to the delight of the *Nation*, France's new rulers included four journalists and four barristers: proof that the printing press could, as the *Nation* was wont to claim, 'shake empires and dethrone kings'.[59]

From 1 April, the paper carried a regular column headed 'The Irish Revolution', joined a week later by 'Easy Lessons in Military Matters by a Veteran' ('How to Make a Pike, How to Pull

FIGURE 25 Thomas Francis Meagher

a Dragoon from His Horse, How to Try and Buy a Rifle'). Further upheavals in Italy, Hungary, and Bohemia were followed with equally breathless interest, and a further escalation of language. Meagher, the privileged son of a quintessentially O'Connellite politician and businessman in Waterford, adopted French-republican trappings and shaped them to the Irish style learned from the *Nation*'s ballads: shackles, tyrants, freemen, the cannon's liberating roar, and above all the sword, on which he made a classic speech. His account of his final embrace of a revolutionary démarche, as he left his rich father's comfortable house on the tree-lined Mall in Waterford on a summer evening, is a classic summation of revolutionary Romanticism: Mrs Carlyle's prediction come true at last. It it also movingly anticipates the conflicts immortalized in Turgenev's *Fathers and Sons* fourteen years later, or Tancredi's departure from his uncle's palazzo to join the Garibaldian forces in Lampedusa's *The Leopard*.

I ran up to the drawing-room, where my father and aunt were
sitting at the time, to wish them good-bye. I put on my tri-col-
our sash—green, white and orange—buckled on my sword-belt,
cross-belt, cartouche box, and flourishing a very handsome old
sword, which belonged to a granduncle of mine in the days of
the Merchant Corps of the Waterford Volunteers...gave myself
up to the gay illusion of a gallant fight, a triumphal entry, at the
head of thousands into Dublin before long. I was full of liveli-
ness and hope at that moment, and welcomed the struggle with
a laughing heart. But, I recollect it well, my father was far otherwise. He seemed to me mournfully serious, and impressed with
the saddest anticipation.[60]

His father had good cause. The government had at once anticipated and exacerbated the final adoption of the Sword, by arresting John Mitchel in March and convicting him of treason-felony.
In July the more moderate Duffy, along with several others, was
also arrested. He was tried for high treason the following February, when a blatantly packed jury just failed to convict him;
for all the administration's efforts a retrial proved no more decisive and he was eventually released. This 'hideous farce' gave his
friend Thomas Carlyle great agonies of mind. 'I hope he always
believes there is no honest thing I could do to help him which
it would not be a pleasure to me to attempt,' he wrote to John
O'Hagan. His friend was still 'the brave Duffy, whom I always
love'; from Chelsea, Carlyle denounced the 'set of laws and practices, disowned by heaven and on earth productive of Skibbereen
Unions, Liberation O'Connells, and the exile of Ireland's bravest
sons'. This last phrase was worthy of the *Nation* at its most fer-
vent, and suggests Carlyle had indeed been reading the journal;

while the Skibbereen reference shows that he was sharply aware of one of the most scandalous and horrifying locations of Famine starvation. And it reminds us that several of those 'bravest sons of Ireland', now heading for exile, had been his disciples.[61]

The hopeless rising led by a late Young Ireland recruit, William Smith O'Brien, followed in July. It fixed Young Ireland in the English mind not as Carlylean Romantics but as savage Milesian revolutionaries, of the kind forecast by Carlyle in 1839. Meagher's revolutionary invocations expressed the *Nation*'s version of Irish history, past and future, and anticipated that of Patrick Pearse:

> The work begun by the Norman shall never be completed. Generation transmits to generation the holy passion. From the blood which drenched the scaffolds of 1798, the felons of this year have sprung [loud cheers]. Should their blood flow—peace, and loyalty, and debasement, may here for a time, resume their reign— the snows of a winter, the flowers of a summer, may clothe the proscribed graves—but from those graves there shall be a resurrection [loud cheers].[62]

But the failed rebellion showed the metropolitan Irish intelligentsia that the supercharged expectations of the *Nation* had not been altogether representative of feeling in the country at large, especially among those sections of the population intent only on survival.

The 'felons' who led the 1848 Rising, or were convicted of inciting it, did not mount the scaffold, being mostly transported abroad. Duffy refloated the *Nation* and stayed on in Ireland for several years, briefly becoming an MP in the early 1850s, when

FIGURE 26 The Carlyles at home in Chelsea, 1858

he pressed hard for tenant reform. During his London sojourns he frequented the Carlyles' Chelsea house; they not only offered constant hospitality but helped him to furnish his own lodgings with, symbolically, a set of Carlyle's old book-cases.[63] Carlyle contributed briefly to Duffy's *Nation* and stayed close to him. In 1849 he even—to the fury of the Lord-Lieutenant, Clarendon— instigated a tour of Ireland in the company of the accused fel-on.[64] The Chelsea sage's recollection of this odd journey was posthumously published in 1882.[65] It constitutes one of those texts by which his racist attitudes towards the Irish are judged, and it is certainly violently prejudiced and despairing. He came back convinced there was no 'remedy for Ireland' except to 'cease following the devil: no other remedy I can see'. Just after return-ing to Britain he wrote a violent letter to Emerson suggesting

FIGURE 27 Carlyle, a photograph signed
in Limerick, 24 July 1849

the surplus Irish poor should be blackleaded and exported to
the plantations.[66] In the same year he wrote his notorious 'Occasional Discourse on the Negro Question'.

This is the racist Carlyle familiar to later generations: the connection between his attitudes to the Irish and the West Indians
is swiftly—too swiftly—made. But his rueful affection for the
Romantic Young Irelanders and his attempts to preach redemption to Ireland (even through the pages of the *Nation*) mean that
simply equating his views with those of Robert Knox's Saxonist
racial superiority (controversial even in their day) does not fully
answer the case. He had always seen the causes of Irish degradation as misrule, oppression, and the hopeless economics of absentee landlordism and potato dependency. Threatening and sinister
as they are, 'These poor Celtiberian Irish brothers, what can *they*
help it? They cannot stay at home, and starve. It is just and natural that they come hither as a curse on us.'[67] When he suggests

as alternatives improvement or extermination, the latter clearly means starvation and emigration, not genocide: nor is he advocating these expedients. 'We are married to Ireland by the Ground-plan of this world', he had told Duffy: 'a thickskinned labouring man to a drunken ill-tongued wife: and dreadful family quarrels have ensued!'[68] Ireland, as so often, is feminized here, but hardly racialized. Nevertheless, like the more obviously sympathetic Sidney Smith in the *Edinburgh Review*, Carlyle judged the Irish as self-destructive, unreliable, vehement—qualities that might infect the English. 'The Irish population must get itself redressed and saved, for the sake of the English if nothing else.'[69] For all his friendship with Duffy, the *Reminscences* of his Irish journey in 1849 suggest grimmer implications. Still, Duffy's own impressions of the West of Ireland in 1849 would be called racist if they had been written by Carlyle:

> I have seen in the streets of Galway crowds of creatures more debased than the yahoos of Swift—creatures having only a distant and hideous resemblance to human beings. Grey-headed old men, whose idiot faces had hardened into a settled leer of mendicancy, simeous and semi-human; and women filthier and more frightful than the harpies, who, at the jingle of a coin on the pavement, swarmed in myriads from unseen places, struggling, screaming, shrieking for their prey, like some monstrous and unclean animals.[70]

It was traumatic for both of them. But Carlyle's post-Famine visit had been impelled by his belief that Ireland, 'a country scourged by angry Gods...demanded to be seen and heard; is one of the notablest spots in the whole world just now'.[71] His letters

THE VILLAGE OF TULLIG.

FIGURE 28 An Irish village towards the end of the Famine, 1849

show an increasing horror as he travels into the ravaged countryside and a mounting repellence towards 'the repeal population'; unsurprisingly, he regretted Duffy's political relationship to
them. But his chief denunciations were reserved for Irish elites
and he also believed that the signs of improvement were there,
bringing Ireland up to the English level. 'My surprise...has
rather been of the joyful kind: that of finding *more* good men,
of all descriptions, busy in their places, and more germs of hope
and benefit, discoverable in this waste scene of Human Distrac-
tions and Delusions, than I had dared to anticipate.' In the end he
hoped for 'the possibility of a new Ireland (which ought to mean
a new England and a new Scotland)'.[72] This optimistic message,
directed at the English governors of Ireland, was probably also
intended to rehabilitate Duffy in the eyes of officialdom. It did
not work, but Duffy remained a friend and defender of Carlyle
all his life.

And what a life it was. The foreign futures of the Irish Romantics, after the dizzying 1840s, are as striking and dramatic as their Irish pasts. Mitchel, the ur-Carlylean, became an influential journalist in America and a passionate pro-slaver and supporter of the South in the Civil War. His writings, such as *Jail Journal* and *The Last Conquest of Ireland (Perhaps)*, would have as much influence on Irish republican ideology as *The Spirit of the Nation* (a distillation of the newspaper's choicest productions) had upon the Young Ireland generation. Meagher also pursued a spectacular career in American politics, becoming a celebrated Civil War general and then Governor of Montana, before disappearing mysteriously off a Missouri paddleboat. Darcy McGee embraced a new life as a founding father of Canadian federation; his repudiation of republican nationalism earned him assassination by an American Fenian. Doheny, Dillon, Martin, and others too numerous to mention similarly flourished in the New World, destination of so many heroes in the fiction of the Romantic era. Their dramatic trajectories belong in novels by Victor Hugo or operas by Berlioz, and their lives indeed found their way into fiction.[73] In a development more reminiscent of Trollope, Thomas O'Hagan stayed at home and became the first Catholic Lord Chancellor of Ireland.

But Gavan Duffy's career is the most arresting of all. Emigrating to Australia in 1855, he became Governor of Victoria and a key figure in Australian federation, retiring with a knighthood. He always retained an eye to Irish politics, and wanted to stand as a Home Rule candidate for Meath in 1875—furious at being passed over for an unknown young landlord called Charles Stewart Parnell. (He would later tangle with Parnell at several points during the 1880s.[74]) He wrote copious and invaluable contemporary histories and memoirs, with titles like *My Life in Two Hemispheres*, having learned in his Young Ireland days the importance of capturing the historical narrative. Eventually he returned to live in the South of France in 1892, whence he involved himself in the politics of the Irish cultural revival, trying to reignite his Library of Ireland and becoming embroiled—as will be seen—in a titanic struggle with the ambitious young W. B. Yeats.

Duffy's autobiography was well named *My Life in Two Hemispheres*. The Irish Romantics inhabited several worlds, overlapping and sometimes contradicting each other, rather like the contemporary Russian avatars written about so well by E. H. Carr and Isaiah Berlin. And Romanticism in Ireland conditioned several kinds of national consciousness, not all of them 'nationalist' in the accepted sense. One might, in considering unexpected futures, look forward to the future career of Isaac Butt, who would play John the Baptist to Parnell's Messiah— and become a close friend of John Butler Yeats, father of the future poet.[75] Samuel Ferguson, once hailed by the *Nation* as a proto-nationalist, followed another course. But though he retreated to the comfortable worlds of antiquarian scholarship and grand Dublin life, he too lived on just long enough to intersect with the opening of W. B. Yeats's literary career. So for that matter did Speranza, Lady Wilde. The young men and women of the 1830s and 1840s not only experienced a complex, optimistic moment of Irish experience which awaits its literary history; they were also important shaping influences in the much more celebrated Literary Revival of the *fin de siècle*.

Current criticism tends to read the effusive literary productions of this era through themes such as the picaresque, or racial 'othering', or a colonized discourse which can be paralleled elsewhere in the British Empire. It might be more profitable to look at what the Irish Romantics wanted to do, what they thought they were doing, whom they admired, and how they expressed their nationalism, or sense of nationality. The Young Irelanders wanted to write fiction and poetry which would forge a national consciousness. So did Samuel Ferguson, Isaac Butt, and others on the opposite political side. Both enterprises were preoccupied with the place of Protestants in the new post-Emancipation Catholic Ireland. Both also wanted to discover (or create) an Irish Ossian and out-Scott Scott. Ferguson's epic poem *Congal*, using O'Donovan's 1842 saga translations but not published till 1872, sustains this theme; so do the Carlylean history-epics of Standish O'Grady, which appeared around the same time. And these texts, written by Protestant Unionists determined to claim an Irish identity, were key influences on the young Yeats.

Carlyle's continuing influence can also be discerned in the way that Mitchel and Duffy wrote history, and the galvanic effect they wanted it to have. The moment of Protestant Repeal in 1848 crystallized a point in time when the agenda of Ferguson and Butt appeared to converge with that of Davis, Duffy, and Mitchel.[76] Perhaps what we also see at this juncture is the final expression of the reconciliatory agenda of Irish literature in the first decade of the Union, discussed in the last chapter. But by the 1840s Italy rather than Scotland seemed an appropriate comparator for Ireland: 'her land so fair, her soul so fiery, her glories so remote, her sorrow so deep, and her slavery so unending... Who in Italy doubts that the next war (if nothing sooner) will hurl the aliens from her frontier? Who here doubts that Ireland, too, waits but for some crisis to achieve her liberty?'[77] And in 1848 France suggested another model again. When this did not work, Meagher, from American exile, berated his insufficiently revolutionary countrymen as corrupt Venetians.

> The fate of Venice is your fate. Your country has passed from your hands. The curse of Falieri [*recte* Faliero] has crossed from the Adriatic—it is here fulfilled:
>
>> She shall be bought
>> And sold, and be an appanage to those
>> Who shall despise her.[78]

For all the political energy expressed by the Irish literary world in the 1830s and 1840s, the expectation of reform and revolution ended in disruption and dispersal. The moment of apparent convergence masked a general shift from inclusive to exclusive attitudes in nationalism, despite Davis's efforts. One view of this era posits an inevitably racialized, dictatorial, colonialist process, where Davis's and Ferguson's notions of mobilizing Protestants in the national interest appear a well-meaning delusion, while the fiction of Lever and Carleton colludes in an essentially racist process of representing the 'other'. But such a reading leaves unexplored the complexity of Carlyle's influence on Irish Romanticism, the contradictions of his own attitudes towards Ireland, the intentions of the *Nation*'s contributors, the intersections with their Protestant and Unionist counterparts, and the ambiguities of their ambitions within the Empire as well as outside it. It is worth recapturing the expectations of the 1830s and early 1840s as a way of understanding the mentality of the first Romantics—and to suggest that the irruption of the Famine, and the ensuing radicalization of nationalist politics, produced an unexpected effect, creating barriers and divergences which were not, up to that point, inevitable.

Above all, more of the literary culture of Irish Romanticism survived to influence the later Literary Revival than is often recognized. The rhetoric of Young Ireland helped construct, by reaction, the styles forged so differently by Yeats, Synge and Joyce. When Yeats, in old age, wrote of his contemporaries Synge and Gregory

> We were the last Romantics—chose for theme
> Traditional sanctity and loveliness;
> Whatever's written in what poets name
> The book of the people...[79]

he knew that there had been First Romantics before him, whose efforts to construct a tradition which could incorporate nationally minded Protestants prefigured the projects of his own generation. Of the Young Irelanders he wrote: 'They were not separated individual men; they spoke or tried to speak out of a people to a people; behind them stretched the generations.'[80] This continuity lay behind much of his own early enterprise. It is time now to turn to supernatural and esoteric themes in nineteenth-century Irish writing, about which exactly the same might be said.

3

Lost in the Big House: Anglo-Irishry and
the Uses of the Supernatural

A boy sits with his father before a fire in the library of a Big
House in Ireland on a winter's evening. 'Of the date of the
house,' the narrator tells us, 'I can tell you nothing accurate. It
was built by a forebear of ours who was a historical character,
but it is just about that time that the history of Ireland begins to
be fabulous, so that it is truer to tell you merely that the house
was very old.' They are alone in the house except for a couple
of servants. The boy is trembling with suppressed excitement
because he has been told that grey-lag geese have arrived on
the nearby bog and he longs to go shooting the next day. The
father has other things on his mind; he has as usual gone round
the house fastening every window and door. ' "You never know
who might come over the bog." And certainly on the other side
of the bog there were hills of which we knew nothing.' And
he has long ago told his son that, when they are sitting in that
room at night, if he ever instructs him to go over and 'Look at
the picture', a Dutch landscape hanging on the panelled wall, he

must do just that and not turn around. As the boy sits drinking his milk, these long-expected words are uttered. He obediently stands facing the wall; the only door into the room opens and four tall men walk in. They have come to shoot his father. But though their quarry could not have left by the door, he has magically disappeared. The huge house is searched, unavailingly; the men threaten to burn it, but the boy knows they will not, because it contains a relic of the True Cross, given to the family by 'one of the popes'. Instead they make him swear on the relic that he believes his father is still in the house, the assassins kneeling devoutly throughout. As he does so, spinning it out, he hears the sounds of a horse being walked softly across the stable yard and finally trotting down the avenue. The men from the bog hear the horse only when it is galloping down the road to safety. The boy will never see his father again. As they leave, he asks one of the men about shooting geese. The chapter ends:

> To look at him you would have said that he was the worst of the four, and yet he told me little things about shooting that are pure gold to a boy; and when he saw how keen I was on the geese, he said to me just as they all went out through the door: 'And a goose takes a long time to get his pace up. Don't aim so much in front of a goose as you do at other birds.'
>
> And when they'd all gone he opened the door again and put his head inside, and said, word for word as I write it: 'And if it ever comes to it, and God knows the world's full of trouble, aim a foot in front of a man walking, at a hundred yards.'[1]

Few novels begin as well as this one, but the reason why it may be unfamiliar to a wide readership is that it collapses into an unresolved mish-mash of prophecies, obscure politics, unconvincing love-affairs, and ultimate irresolution. It is called *The Curse of the Wise Woman*, and is by the Irish fantasy-writer Lord Dunsany, who published it in 1933. Late though it is, that first chapter seems to contain the essence of the Anglo-Irish Big House novel: loneliness, uncertainty, a solitary house in an implicitly threatening countryside, unknown natives, the threat of death. There is also, as so often in the genre, a missing or dead mother.

Several of these elements are established early in post-Union fiction: by the early 1840s, baroque Ascendancy fears of the threatening world beyond the demesne wall had become a cliché to be satirized in Trollope's *The Kellys and the O'Kellys*. That first chapter of the Dunsany novel also builds in elements from folktales: there is a secret room (how do you think the father disappeared?), and an injunction that must not be disobeyed. And, along with this, we intuit an odd complicity with those very natives: an understanding of the country and its ways, by which means the narrator reassures himself of his 'place' in the Irish scheme of things; a supernatural element which is also, in its way, a shared possession. Dunsany himself was a Plunkett—a Catholic family of 'Old English', rather than Cromwellian, origin. This gives the relationship to the other world a particular spin. But all the other elements conjure up Maturin's *Melmoth the Wanderer* or Sheridan Le Fanu's *Uncle Silas*, and the whole tradition of nineteenth-century Gothic. The no less threatening present—the early 1930s—is adroitly indicated as well: the men from the bog carry 'long, single-barrelled pistols, old even then; nothing like the automatics they use nowadays'.[2]

Dunsany was a minor writer of the late Revival, nowadays mainly remembered as an associate of Yeats. They were closely connected for a while, through the Abbey Theatre and in other ways, but ended by hating each other vehemently; by 1933, if Dunsany had been able to aim his gun a foot in front of Yeats walking, he would probably have jumped at the chance.[3] By then, too, the Irish Big House novels were a very well-established genre, and they have continued to attract critical attention. Most of the key works date from the century after 1880—when the Land War of 1879–82 began a process that definitively changed the position of the Ascendancy landlords. This is true of the classic Big House novels such as *A Drama in Muslin* by George Moore (1886), *The Real Charlotte* by Somerville and Ross (1894),

FIGURE **29** Lisselane, West Cork, home of the Bence-Jones family, under armed guard during the Land War, 1880

The Last September by Elizabeth Bowen (1929), *Mount Prospect* by Elizabeth O'Connor (Una Troy) (1936), *The Gates* by Jennifer Johnston (1973), *Good Behaviour* by Molly Keane (1981), and *Fools of Fortune* by William Trevor (1983).[4] The previous generation of Ascendancy fiction involves—like those later novels—a mansion and its inhabitants outliving their time. But the pre-1880 Irish Big House novel is more penetratingly infused with the idea of history as a haunting, and with the notion of a continuing past of unease and insecurity, often implying guilt and repression.

So far, so Gothic. The tradition of Big House novels relates easily to a linked genre—nineteenth-century Irish Gothic, involving family secrets, disputed inheritances, uncertain descents, sexual corruption, and threatening elements of the supernatural. The fiction of Gothic horror has been analysed by many authorities in terms of a fear of the return of feudalism; and—particularly in English Gothic fiction—the exotic, almost seductive, phantom of revived Catholicism.[5] This might seem to have its Irish relevance, though the spectre of Ireland is curiously downplayed in most treatments of the English horror-novel. The traditions of Irish fiction from the 1830s, briefly considered in the last chapter, often employ supernatural stratagems as a way of responding to history; Isaac Butt, that emblematic figure slipping unreliably between politics and literature, is one example, with his necromantic approach to the past and its evidences. His language when debating Repeal of the Union against Daniel O'Connell in 1843 is striking:

> let the memories of past wrongs be forgotten; away with the evil
> spirit that would wander among the tombs, to hold commun-
> ion only with the evil things of other days, and by an infernal

necromancy call from the grave the hideous spectres of forgotten crimes to disturb the present generation with the guilt and passions of the past.[6]

Political and literary language collide in occult imagery. The images in early writings of Butt, such as his short story set in Trinity College, 'The Murdered Fellow', invoke guilty secrets, threatening Catholicism, and a Faustian bargain. This is yet more true, as will be seen, for his early associate Sheridan Le Fanu.

But the implications of nineteenth-century Irish fiction also present problems for the literary historian. How does it relate to the idea that the growth of nationalism necessarily employs the vehicle of fictional narrative in imagining a national community? This is an attractive idea when applied to certain societies (England, America, France) but more problematic for others. Irish novels do not fit this function very readily. In Ireland, history-writing may supply that bonding cement rather than fiction.[7] That suggestive subtitle 'national tale' can lead to oversimplified assumptions about mid-century fiction and nationalist belief. We might think of Scottish contrasts and parallels. If the national tale fizzles out after the 1830s, Scots fiction devolves into a literature which celebrates the Kailyard on one side and produces wholesome fare by Stevenson and Buchan on another. (Hogg haunts them as much as Scott does.) Meanwhile Irish novelists withdraw into a traumatized space where they negotiate with historical guilt, in fictions set in houses which symbolize the architecture of an authority based on dispossession.[8] But this seems too simple. As regards Scotland, one might point out that Stevenson's and Buchan's novels are hard to categorize, being shot through

with Irish-style ambivalences, doublings and supernatural associations. And regarding Ireland's supposed contrast to Scotland
under the Union, recent historiography has emphasized an Irish
imperializing energy, where young middle-class Catholics, fast-
tracked in the necessary examinations by the new Queen's Col-
leges, took themselves off to the Empire and ran bits of it as to
the manner born, just like their Scottish contemporaries. They
even wrote popular fictions about it.[9] This is one of the many
ways in which post-Famine Ireland is as much about modernization as stasis. It suggests the world reflected in Trollope's Irish
novels (apart from the deliberately pessimistic first and last—*The
Macdermots of Ballycloran* and *The Landleaguers*), which span the
period from 1840 to 1880.

When from the mid 1880s the young Yeats would come to
look at the literary inheritance left to him by the previous generation, he would concentrate on the fiction of Carleton and the
Banims, searching for a rough-hewn realism that would inscribe
national truths in what he memorably called a 'fiery shorthand'.
It is doubtful if he knew that his father's friend Isaac Butt wrote
novels, and he does not mention Le Fanu a great deal, though
he certainly read him.[10] But in considering the literary world
he came into, it is necessary to revisit the part that supernaturalism and religion plays in the Anglo-Irish imagination in the
nineteenth century. And when we see that two key elements in
this involve Swedenborgianism and fairy belief, the relevance to
Yeats's inheritance can hardly be doubted.

If Ireland in the second half of the nineteenth century was
indeed a modernizing society, the connections to an interest in
the supernatural are worth examining. The dichotomy between

a 'traditional' and a 'modern' world-view is now generally agreed to be so crude as to be misleading. Jeremy Bentham's notion that modern forms of communication, and particularly the daily newspaper, drive out superstition is striking: 'before this talisman not only devils but ghosts, vampires, witches and all their kindred tribes are driven out of the land, never to return again, for the touch of holy water is not as intolerable to them as the bare smell of printer's ink.'[11] Had he lived to see the cult of nineteenth-century popular horror-fiction in full flood, Bentham might have thought again; and one of the key books in the phenomenon was the Irishman Bram Stoker's *Dracula* (1897), which derives much of its power from imposing ancient occult horrors on a world of telegraphs, steam-power, shorthand, and electricity.

Angela Bourke has brilliantly demonstrated the connections between a modernizing society in the Ireland of the mid 1890s, exactly when Stoker was writing *Dracula*, and the endurance and uses of fairy faith in her classic study *The Burning of Bridget Cleary* (1999). In fact, the fascination with investigating fairy faith and the interference of malevolent forces had been evident throughout the nineteenth century; it is a dominant theme in the fiction of the Banim brothers. Another early milestone was Thomas Crofton Croker's work in the 1820s. *Fairy Legends and Traditions of the South of Ireland* first appeared in 1825, with a second edition the following year incorporating engravings by his fellow Corkman Daniel Maclise; a third series followed in 1828. Croker, from an influential Protestant family, is an important figure in the antiquarian and folklorist movement of the 1820s and 1830s; like the translators and scholars of Gaelic manuscripts

FIGURE 30 Thomas Crofton
Croker by Daniel Maclise, 1829

in this era, he would help provide the mother-lode of material
mined by cultural revivalists at the end of the century.[12] Croker
collected information on folk culture and rituals, notably the
mourning cry, or *caoine*; his first book, published in 1824, was
called *Researches in the South of Ireland* and is an idiosyncratic
mixture of history, observations, and *vade mecum* for the traveller. It was the subsequent fairy-legend collection that made his
name, in Europe as well as in Ireland and Britain: Jacob Grimm
translated it into German, and Walter Scott enthusiastically pros-
elytized on its behalf.

Croker's presentation of the fairy world is oddly ambiguous.
Maclise's illustrations suggest a kind of pre-Rackham or Greena-
way prettiness and Croker himself invokes Shakespeare in his
conclusion to his first series:

FIGURE 31 *A Fairy Dance* by Daniel Maclise, 1826

The Shefro, the Banshee, and the other creatures of imagination who bear them company, now take their farewell of the reader. As knowledge advances, they recede and vanish, as the mists of the valley melt into air beneath the beams of the morning sun.

When rational education shall be diffused among the misguided peasantry of Ireland, the belief in such supernatural beings must disappear in that country, as it has done in England, and these 'shadowy tribes' will live only in books. The Compiler is therefore not without hope that his little Volume, which delivers the legends faithfully as they have been collected from the mouths of the peasantry, may be regarded with feelings of interest.

And now, gentle reader, permit the 'tiny folk', at parting, to address thee in the words of their British kindred, after their revels through 'the Midsummer Night's Dream':

If we shadows have offended
Think but this (and all is mended)
That you have but slumber'd here
While these visions did appear:
And this weak and idle theme
No more yielding but a dream.
Gentles, do not reprehend;
If you pardon, we will mend.[13]

The agenda of modernization, stadial progression, and indeed Unionism could hardly be more clearly delineated. But, despite this attempt at making superstition inoffensive and harmless, there is a powerful malevolent subtext. For instance, Croker points out that fairies are used by the superstitious to rationalize murder, which he sees as a particular deformation of the Munster peasantry: those threatening men from the bog with guns, again. His compilations had a long life, and form the vital background to the later collections of William and Jane Francesca Wilde, and eventually Douglas Hyde, whose 1890 folktale collection *Beside the Fire* is the summation of the process and was a great influence on Yeats's *Celtic Twilight*. (Academic Celtologists in other countries, such as Henri d'Arbois de Jubainville, saw Hyde and other Irish folklorists as disreputable in scholarly terms, but this would not have bothered the young Yeats.) There are elements here of the Romantic primitivism which would fuel other aspects of the Literary Revival at the *fin de siècle*, and which might be seen as a particularly Ascendancy inclination: this approach sustained a much longer shelf-life in literature than in anthropology.[14] Rural popular culture, as first prospected by Croker, would be built into the rediscovery and assertion of an individual national identity at the end of the century. And in this long process from the 1820s to the early 1900s, most of the prominent figures engaged in the exercise of reclamation were Ascendancy Protestants exploring the other side, indeed the 'otherness', of their country.

The importance of supernatural interests to the mindset of the Irish Ascendancy has developed its own historiography. Twenty years ago I suggested some patterns behind the attraction of the occult for Irish Protestant writers—a way of tackling one of the more daunting aspects of Yeats's thought. Rather than simplified Freudianism, the *Unheimlich*, and cruder sociological readings, it seemed more profitable to relate Yeats back to Le Fanu and forward to Elizabeth Bowen, and to discuss the complexity of Ascendancy attitudes towards Catholicism and 'country people', and the way fairy belief mediated this. From this perspective,

> ...the line of Irish Protestant supernatural fiction is an obvious one...It leads from Maturin and Le Fanu to Bram Stoker and Elizabeth Bowen and Yeats—marginalized Irish Protestants all, often living in England but regretting Ireland, stemming from families with strong clerical and professional colorations, whose occult preoccupations surely mirror a sense of displacement, a loss of social and psychological integration, and an escapism motivated by the threat of a takeover by the Catholic middle classes—a threat all the more inexorable because it is being accomplished by peaceful means and with the free legal aid of British governments. The supernatural theme of a corrupt bargain recurs again. Indeed, a strong theme in Protestant gothic is a mingled repulsion and envy where Catholic magic is concerned.[15]

Folklore and anthropological interests merged with occult investigations—not just in the case of Yeats—in order to open a way
into national tradition from a marginalized base, and a claim on
intuitive, organic, traditional forms of wisdom. This involved
reading *Dracula* as an Irish text, mingling guilt, occultism, threatening Big Houses, and Catholic magic. (There is an early connection between Yeats and Stoker through Edward Dowden,
a Trinity don who wrote distinguished studies of Shelley and
Shakespeare and was a mentor to both young men.) In recent
years a number of scholars have considered the question of the
Anglo-Irish and supernaturalism, often invoking Count Dracula
as the inheritor of Ascendancy guilt.[16] But in many of the discussions of the Irish Ascendancy and occult imaginings, the idea
of Protestant insecurity and self-interrogation—which is vital—
has been demoted. The idea of self-conscious historical guilt and
repression has been advanced: in one analysis the Count and his
earth-boxes have been equated with an Irish landlord clinging
on to his illegitimately won territory, while he sucks the blood
of his tenants. In another, more manic treatment the heroine's
name 'Mina' is related to 'Wilhemina', denoting Orange politics and Williamite dispossessions, while 'Dracula' supposedly
derives from *droch-fhola*, allegedly the Gaelic for bad blood.[17] In
this process, Stoker has become progressively Hibernicized, and
Le Fanu forgotten, to the extent that an easy reference can be
made to Stoker's 'dominance in later nineteenth-century Irish
fiction'.[18] However, he did not have a dominant position in Irish,
or any other, fiction in the late nineteenth century: the extraordinary history of *Dracula*'s dominance was yet to come, and would

FIGURE 32 Bram Stoker in 1884

operate through other channels (notably celluloid), exercising its potent effect outside the sphere of Irish cultural history.

Stoker was indeed Irish, from a distinguished Dublin middle-class Protestant family, full of achievers in the worlds of medicine and law. But he wrote only one novel set in Ireland, *The Snake's Pass*—a later version of the 'national tale', with an English–Irish symbolic marriage, much about agrarian improvement, and an evil gombeen-man borrowed straight from Carleton. One of the novel's fans was Stoker's acquaintance and Lyceum Theatre *habitué*, Gladstone. As this might indicate, Stoker was a fixture in London society. He lived his whole adult life in England, as Henry Irving's invaluable manager and a great figure in theatre-land; even his holidays were spent in Scotland and (of course) Whitby. An Irish conditioning, and even an escape from Ireland, may nonetheless be encoded in his one great novel: the Gothic imagination works by indirection and repression. But it is more relevant to see *Dracula* as inflected by contemporary analysts of degeneration and the hidden psyche such as Lombroso, Nordau, Charcot, all specifically invoked in the novel. It teems with ideas of degeneracy, the subconscious, sexual instability, and racial insecurity. There is also a powerful theme of Anglo-American imperialism, and the fashionable mania for the Balkans. Stoker's copious notes for the book survive, listing sources such as studies of Romania, Hungary, the Carpathians, Transylvania, dream theory, and much else: but nothing Irish.[19] The Irishman John Anster's translation of *Faust* is the closest thing to an Irish influence: Irving played Faust in 1885, a huge success in which Stoker was much involved, and the Faust story has a particular resonance for Irish Ascendancy literature. The nearest local folklore Stoker apparently consulted was Welsh, though admittedly he may have read Lady Wilde.[20] In many ways *Dracula* reads more like John Buchan on mescaline than anything Irish. Its primary identity is as English (or British) shocker rather than Anglo-Irish meditation—however wittily the Count and his earth-boxes may be interpreted as a metaphor for declining Irish landlords. (Stoker was, of course, very far from being a landlord and his family had nothing to do with Big Houses.[21]) And while the idea of Van Helsing's Catholic white magic is striking, Jonathan Harker puts on his crucifix with a tremor as an 'Englishman'.

However, even with this balance restored, vampires have particularly Irish resonances, and Stoker may well indeed have first been exposed to them through Dowden's work on the Shelley circle. John Polidori's *The Vampyre* was followed by subsequent shockers like *Varney the Vampire*—a craze that was exacerbated

FIGURE 33 The restrained
first edition of *Dracula*, 1897

by the 1850 English translation of Augustin Calmet's *The Phantom World*. This was the route whereby bloodsuckers became an image used by Irish writers, including Dion Boucicault (*The Vampire*, 1852) and even William Carleton. The prime Irish example is, however, Sheridan Le Fanu, with *Carmilla* (an 1872 vampire novella set in an Austrian castle) long predating *Dracula*.[22] Moreover, the idea of a Northern European magus, in the form of Stoker's Van Helsing, probably comes from Sheridan Le Fanu's narrator in his ghost stories, Dr Hesselius. Stoker's far more famous creation belongs in a certain Irish tradition. But the uses of the supernatural for the Irish Protestant imagination can be more richly explored through the ghost stories of Sheridan Le Fanu, and particularly his masterpiece, the novel *Uncle Silas*.

Le Fanu was one of the young Tory intellectuals grouped around Isaac Butt's *Dublin University Magazine* in the 1830s: he actually became its proprietor and editor in 1861. In the interim

FIGURE 34 Sheridan Le Fanu,
c. 1843

he attempted a fling with politics, but, unlike his friend Butt, did not succeed; his wife's early death precipitated a remorseful depression which seems to have lasted off and on for much of his life, and he lived for long periods in gloomy semi-seclusion in Merrion Square. Like Butt and Ferguson, he was briefly radical-ized by the British government's appalling failure to combat the Irish famine, and he supported John Mitchel's and T. F. Meagh-er's denunciation of government policy—though not, unsurpris-ingly, their eventual protest in arms. Unlike Stoker, he remained a Dubliner all his life; unlike Stoker, he was related closely to the world of grandee Ascendancy landlords (in his case the Duf-ferins). The conditions of his family background, his Huguenot inheritance, his role in Dublin life, are vital to his imagination; like Samuel Ferguson, he was preoccupied with the architecture of the city, and with its history and development. Early historical novels like *The Fortunes of Colonel Torlogh O'Brien*, *The Cock and Anchor*, and especially *The House by the Churchyard* create surreal historical conjunctions which anticipate Flann O'Brien, and strongly influenced Joyce (who took the Chapelizod setting of *The House by the Churchyard* for *Finnegans Wake*, and peppered his novel with allusions to Le Fanu's work).

Le Fanu represents an important chapter in the story of the Anglo-Irish preoccupation with an imagined eighteenth century, a theme which looks back to Owenson and forward to Yeats; but above all he retains his importance as a novelist of the uncanny. For all his grand connections, and the marvellous evocations of gloomy country houses which inhabit his fiction, Le Fanu's use of supernaturalism is more closely connected to theological uncertainty than to landlord guilt. This is strikingly reflected in his use of Swedenborgianism. The early eighteenth-century mystic Emmanuel Swedenborg moved from a scientific background to a world of revelation, where he believed that access to the dimension of angels was possible through concentration and self-application: an 'inner eye' could be opened in order to access a whole universe of correspondences, where the imperfections of the everyday would be traded in for their angelic archetypes. *Heaven and Hell* (1758) is a sort of occult guidebook to this other world, with direct, rather laconic instructions on how to manipulate these mutations. In some ways Swedenborg was a classic eighteenth-century magus, in others an early reaction against the Enlightenment—in which role he represents an important

FIGURE 35 Emmanuel
Swedenborg by
Per Krafft, 1766

influence on European literary Romanticism. He is also deeply
embroiled in scriptural exegesis, much inspired by the Revelation
of Saint John the Divine. The domain of spirits is intermediate
between Heaven and Hell; its denizens occupy it pending reas-
signment. But if it is possible to access the dimension of Heaven
and walk with angels, it is also possible to travel in the other
direction. Hell is a permanent and surrounding presence, exca-
vated directly below our everyday life, and actually occupied by
many of us without realizing it. And the Lord rules it as well as
Heaven.

Swedenborg's influence on Blake was intermittently powerful,
and Yeats would later inherit this. But in between these literary
followers of the magus came the work of Le Fanu. *Uncle Silas*
(1864) conjures up a world of symbols, doubling, and suggestions

of access into other worlds. These are contained within the confines of a novel which, unlike the short stories, more or less resolves itself without needing any supernatural explanations. It is in its way a Gothic horror-story, but written with an oddly effective economy and power. The heroine, Maud Ruthyn, goes to her uncle's Great House, Bartram-Haugh, when her strange father dies; her fantasies of happiness are corroded by its atmosphere and the reappearance of threatening figures from her youth. As the atmosphere closes in, she becomes the instrument and object of dark forces determined to destroy her, concentrated into the extraordinary figure of her uncle. W. J. McCormack convincingly presents the novel as a Swedenborgian parable, with Maud's uncle and father doubled (rather like the witch and the mother in Freudian versions of 'Hansel and Gretel'). Some critics see Swedenborgianism in the novel as 'threatening', which is odd, as it provides the resolution in a last paragraph which could read like a paragraph from Swedenborg's own *Heaven and Hell*. 'The world', we are told by the redeemed and rescued Maud, 'is a parable—the habitation of symbols—the phantoms of spiritual things immortal shown in material shape. May the blessed second-sight be mine—to recognize under these beautiful forms of earth the ANGELS who wear them; for I am sure we may walk with them if we will, and hear them speak.'[23]

Uncle Silas, it has been said by one of its most perceptive analysts, is a novel of 'pressure, volume and spiritual urgency which make it comparable to *Wuthering Heights*'. That critic, significantly, was Elizabeth Bowen, who in a powerful introduction to a 1947 reprint first claimed it as an Irish novel set in a Derbyshire disguise. She was right. It began life as a short story set in Ireland and would have stayed there if Le Fanu's publisher had not dictated otherwise. The appurtenances, the geography, the dialects are English but the atmosphere is Irish—in Bowen's view, because 'it is sexless, and it shows a sublimated infantilism'. Bowen also remarks that *Uncle Silas* 'bristles with symbols', and it certainly does.[24] It is a novel about death: graveyards feature, leading to converse with the departed; Maud's terrifying French governess is constantly portrayed as a grotesque phantom or revenant who lives with the dead.

Anglo-Irish insecurity is undeniably present. But how far it should be seen as symbolizing the guilt of the Anglo-Irish who built Yeats's great gazebo is unproven. And if Bartram-Haugh is a corner of Derbyshire that is forever Ireland, it is hard to see that Le Fanu's vampire novella *Carmilla* belongs anywhere but in Styria, or that her ancestors are any more Irish than Countess Báthory. The countervailing tendency is well established and the imaginative transposition is tempting: to assert that Irish Gothic equals Ascendancy guilt, that the Big House is a location of imprisonment and threat representing Irish history, that the vampire is a particularly Anglo-Irish image for exploitation and demoralization, ingeniously underpinned by the fact that some cartoonists in the late nineteenth century portrayed Fenians as vampire bats. Thus the Styrian lesbian vampire Carmilla allegedly turns into an 'autochthonous manifestation of the female nation, reaching out from portraits and ruined castles to fascinate and destroy the expatriate English, confined, as Laura is in the novella, by a sterile world of patriarchal rationality where no young men are permitted because no continuation is possible'.[25] Perhaps the connections between nation and narration can be taken a step too far.

Le Fanu's supercharged imagery has also inspired an ingenious linkage between the small black monkey which haunts a London clergyman in the story 'Green Tea' and the simianization of the Irish in *Punch* cartoons.[26] But that ape clearly comes from another kind of demonology altogether.

Authorial intention is one thing, and the workings of subconscious symbolism another—especially in Gothic literature. But it is worth asking how self-consciously guilty and insecure the mid-nineteenth-century Protestant Ascendancy actually were. One thinks of John Anster, the poetic translator of *Faust* and a literary star of the *DUM* circle, coming to visit the Le Fanu family in their County Limerick rectory at a time of widespread rural unrest about the enforced payment of tithes by Catholic farmers to Protestant clergy. The visitor's carriage was pursued by an angry crowd as it made its way to its destination; the guest descended unflurried and rather smug, under the impression that he had been followed by a crowd who had recognized him and wanted to congratulate him on his literary genius. 'When we told him what the cheering was, his visage changed.' It had not occurred to the poet that the local people saw the rector as a bloodsucking exploiter—as they clearly did. We may be more conscious of the Ascendancy's need to feel guilt than they were.[27]

On the other hand, this anecdote about Anster reminds us that the Protestant Ascendancy was just that—Protestant; and that religion and religious consciousness penetrated every level of Irish life in the mid nineteenth century. This was especially true after the Protestant evangelical revival from the 1830s, but also before: on his Irish tours Wesley had a particular effect on Irish country-house life. The mid century saw a great outpouring of apocalyptical Protestant writing.[28] *Melmoth the Wanderer*, like *Faust*, is pre-eminently a Protestant parable on the sin of pride. Christian self-scrutiny, theological uncertainties, doctrinal disputes, declining congregations, educational challenges all beset the nineteenth-century Church of Ireland, particularly after the invasive reforms of Whig governments in the 1830s; *Uncle Silas* was published only four years before Gladstone called an election on the question of disestablishing the Church of Ireland, which was effected in 1869. Swedenborgianism, based closely on frantic scriptural exegesis, comes naturally to people immersed in this world; so do the doppelgängers, familiars, correspondences, and symbols of *In a Glass Darkly* and *Uncle Silas*. This was the world inhabited by Le Fanu, by Maturin, by Yeats's ancestors, and by Elizabeth Bowen's forebears. It is perhaps illustrative to remember the story which eerily echoes *Uncle Silas*, written four decades later: Henry James's *The Turn of the Screw*. Once again we find the house, the child, the governess, the revenants: and the unsettling sense that what we are hearing could possibly be a delusion, that the influence of the supernatural may be the function of a repressed imagination. What V. S. Pritchett, another brilliant critic of Le Fanu, wrote about his ghosts is very reminiscent of *The Turn of the Screw*:

> Le Fanu's ghosts are what I take to be the most disquieting of all: the ghosts that can be justified, blobs of the unconscious that have floated up to the surface of the mind, and which are not irresponsible and perambulatory figments of family history, mooning and clanking about in fancy dress. The evil of the justified ghost is not sportive, wilful, involuntary or extravagant. In Le Fanu the fright is that effect follows cause.[29]

The same is true for James. And not only were Henry James's family origins Irish Protestant, only a generation back; his father was also a follower of Swedenborg. Henry James did not share his brother's belief in psychic phenomena (which links William James to Yeats, and which they discussed on the one occasion they met[30]). But in *The Turn of the Screw* he did use that loophole of doubt which his namesake M. R. James saw as Le Fanu's most brilliant stratagem. He also, above all, knew how to manipulate a powerfully introverted psychology.

The psychological insecurity of Protestant mid-Victorian Ireland is striking, and in many ways well founded, but it can be distracting when too readily elided into the threatened world of the Big House. That world would be threatened too, but not until the end of the century.[31] The Big House literature of the twentieth century, as suggested at the beginning of this chapter, relates to the conditions following the seismic Land War of the 1880s and subsequent Land Acts, which transformed the economic position and the social authority enjoyed by the landlord class, and the psychological assumptions upon which they rested. Before this crisis, Ascendancy consciousness does not seem to have lived in the everyday realization or expectation that the roof was about to fall in; the privileges of landownership were taken for granted in most European societies, and their class had lived through the threat of upheaval often enough before. Nor need we assume that many of them felt a subconscious sense that such a fate might be deserved: this idea was restricted to a minority who reacted against the assumptions of their caste, including—if only briefly—the young W. B. Yeats.

The elision from insecurity to guilt is facilitated by the oversimplified assumption that the Ascendancy can be equated with 'the expatriate English'. This may be a useful rhetorical mode for certain purposes, but the Anglo-Irish were very far from seeing themselves as belonging to England. They thought they had a country, and their consciousness remained no less intense as their world increasingly became a part of the past.[32] The concept behind—for instance—Brian Friel's recent play *The Home Place*, set in Victorian Ireland, is that the Ascendancy look across the Irish Sea to their ancestral origins—and even (in this instance) actually possess a 'home place' in Kent, which they apostrophize rhapsodically. This may be a reassuring notion for those who want to turf them out of their Irish holding, but it certainly was not true for the vast majority of Irish landlords, who clung to their land however badly they managed it. The impulse to belong, and to assert a connection with the land, took many forms and rationalizations: one being, of course, the discovery of antiquarianism, archaeology, topography, and history, discussed in the last chapter. And another thread which could connect the Ascendancy to the land beneath them was a proprietorial interest in fairies.

Le Fanu's interests extended not only to eighteenth-century history and metaphysical religion, but to folklore research in the early nineteenth century, especially around the County Limerick area, where his clerical family had their living. His short stories of the 1860s drew on this, with titles such as 'The Child That Went with the Fairies'. They involve spectral familiars, Faustian bargains, and the existence of parallel worlds of 'little people' in the Irish countryside. Swedenborgian belief similarly suggests another world alongside ours, accessible through doors of perception—by means of using a special eye, developed by spiritual exercise. This sits comfortably with the notion of Celtic fairylore, arranged into a symbolic system for analysts of Irish mores such as Crofton Croker and, later, Evans-Wentz.

The version of fairy activity that emerges for Ireland is intriguingly different from those in other Celtic countries. Fairies in Ireland seem closely linked with historical memories of dispossession and invasion and long-ago battles—unlike the fairylore of Wales, which seems to revolve around sexual interference and property crimes, or of Scotland, where religious transgression features largely, along with forms of autonomous political organization.[33] The seventeenth-century Scots clergyman Robert Kirk's *Secret Commonwealth of Elves, Fauns and Fairies* (1691) was a key text here. Interest in it had been sparked by Walter Scott's *Letters on Demonology and Witchcraft* in 1830, and when Nutt published a reprint of the 1815 edition in 1893 it provided Yeats with much material reflected in the second edition of *The Celtic Twilight*. Though Yeats believed the Scots had 'soured' the disposition of their fairies with theology, he was still able chauvinistically to define Scots and Irish fairies against the dull, contrived, *Gemütlich* fairies of English legend.[34] Kirk similarly elided 'Scottish-Irish' beliefs. In Scotland, too, fairies were sometimes identified with aboriginal inhabitants of the country before its mythic invasions, rather than with fallen angels. The general fairy theory sees fairies as the descendants of spirits caught between Earth and Heaven due to some kind of blocked passage: several Irish authorities report hearing this theory from country people, and the celebrated painting *The Fall of the Rebel Angels*, by a young Corkman, Samuel Forde, in the 1820s may be a covert reference to this.[35] In Ireland, however, a special variant of fairy pedigree allows them to be the descendants of ancient inhabitants—even,

FIGURE 36 Samuel Forde, *The Fall of the Rebel Angels*, 1828

defeated natives displaced by invasion.[36] *Pace* Yeats's dismissal of Sassenach fairies, his idea would later be adapted for the purposes of Edwardian nostalgia and local nationalism by English writers such as Rudyard Kipling and Kenneth Grahame.

The interaction between folklore research and nationalism resonates in many European countries from the early nineteenth century onwards—often (as in Ireland, and many Northern European countries) foregrounding hero tales and legends. For Ireland, a culminating point in the early twentieth century was a massive book by W. Y. Evans-Wentz called *The Fairy-Faith in Celtic Countries* (1911). While Evans-Wentz invokes Freud's early writings and E. B. Tylor's anthropology, he does not really need them.[37] His guides had been Douglas Hyde, George Russell, and his friend W. B. Yeats (to whom the book is dedicated). Many of his Irish examples came from Sligo (particularly Rosses Point), conducted there by his Irish friends, and reading between the lines one can infer that his belief in psychic phenomena was related to spiritism (as Yeats called it) rather than to telepathy or subconscious memory.

Evans-Wentz's research into fairylore, which began as doctoral work in Rennes and Oxford, uses Crofton Croker, Hyde, and other previous annalists, as well as years of patient and rather credulous fieldwork. But Irish fairylore sustains a particular, grounded parallelism with the structures of everyday life, as preserved in Evans-Wentz's exegesis and in the more detached, if still vivid, records of the Department of Folklore in University College Dublin. Fairies deal in horses, they milk cows, they drink, smoke, and dance; but their tastes, anathemas, unpredictabilities echo less acceptable sides of life. These incorporate random violence, death, wasting illnesses, abduction, family feuds, anti-social behaviour, sexual interference, illegitimacy, and mental instability. Fairies also move among humans as the undead, or as corrupt angels: providing services on some occasions, on others interfering with everyday life (especially in matters of marriage and parenthood). The rationalizations of human problems thus provided are clear, and Angela Bourke has, again, summed these up most effectively.

> Viewed as a system of interlocking units of narrative, practice and belief, fairy-legend can be compared to a database: a premodern culture's way of storing and retrieving information and knowledge of every kind, from hygiene and childcare to history and geography. Highly charged and memorable images like that

of a woman emerging on a white horse from a fairy dwelling are the retrieval codes for a whole complex of stored information about land and landscape, community relations, gender roles, medicine, and work in all its aspects: tools, materials and techniques. Stories gain verisimilitude, and storytellers keep their listeners' attention, by the density of circumstance they depict, including social relations and the technical details of work. Most stories, however, are constructed around the unexpected, and therefore memorable, happenings in people's lives. Encounters with or interference by the fairies in these stories remind listeners (and readers) of everything in life that is outside human control.[38]

Fairies also represent alternative social hierarchies, rooted in the land. They are, after all, referred to as 'the gentry' and strike

FIGURE 37 William Wilde by J. H. Maguire, 1847

attitudes in ostentatious opposition to clerical authority. (The attraction of all this for W. B. Yeats will be obvious.) There is an echo, in fairy disputations, of the large literature memorializing Saint Patrick's arguments with the pagan heroes of the Fianna—a traditional Irish literary trope which, again, Yeats would take up. The links between Irish fairylore and subversive opinions are very marked; Evans-Wentz was told that the fairies supported the Boers in the South African War and would fight for Ireland if asked. Leprechauns also, apparently, were equipped with special powers for evading the police, an invaluable resource in rural Ireland.[39]

Decades before Evans-Wentz, Sir William Wilde, physician, antiquarian, and folklorist, followed Croker in noting fairy rationalization among country people for everyday diseases, especially wasting and consumption, and mental deficiency: the idea of

FIGURE 38 'Speranza', Lady Wilde
by George Morosini

changeling substitution struck him in particular. Wilde published his *Irish Popular Superstitions* in 1852; thirty-odd years later his widow, famous in her youth as the nationalist poetess Speranza of the *Nation*, used her husband's findings as the basis of two books of fairylore (*Ancient Legends, Mystic Charms and Superstitions of Ireland*, 1887, and *Ancient Cures, Charms and Usages of Ireland*, 1890). Lady Wilde shaped her accounts around recorded narratives, and stressed the uncanny and ghoulish; there is a strong subtext of the horrors of rural Ireland in the grip of the Famine, which she had invoked in her polemical poetry of the 1840s.[40] Her folklore volumes profoundly influenced the young Yeats, and his volume *The Celtic Twilight*, published in 1893; they may also have been read by Bram Stoker, who like Yeats frequented Lady Wilde's shambolic Chelsea salon. Both the Wildes were interested in Transylvanian legends, which may provide a possible link to *Dracula*. But also, like Le Fanu, who was a Dublin neighbour of the Wildes in Merrion Square, they were drawn to Swedenborgianism—particularly Lady Wilde, who apparently undertook a new translation of *Heaven and Hell*, to be called *The Future Life*, but never completed it. This is surely relevant to her comment at the beginning of her second anthology of Irish fairylore:

> All nations and races from the earliest time have held the intuitive belief that mystic beings were always around them, influencing, though unseen, every action of life, and all the forces of nature. They felt the presence of a spirit in the winds, and the waves, and the swaying branches of the forest trees, and in the primal elements of all that exists. Fire was to them the sacred symbol of the divine essence, ever striving towards ascension;

and water, ever seeking a level, was the emblem of the purifica-
tion that should cover all daily life; while in the elemental earth
they reverenced the power that produces all things, and where all
that lives finds a grave, yet also a resurrection.

Thus to the primitive races of mankind the unseen world of
mystery was a vital and vivid reality; the great over-soul of the vis-
ible, holding a mystic and psychic relation to humanity, and ruling
it through the instrumentality of beings who had strange powers
either for good or evil over human lives and actions.[41]

Thus once again we encounter the theme of a parallel world
which can be entered by concentrated mental and spiritual exercise, and whose denizens engage in activities which both mir-
ror and illuminate our own—and affect our destinies. These
ideas were established in a specifically Protestant strain of Irish
thought by the mid nineteenth century. The idea of a thinning
membrane between the living and the dead is linked to explorations of a subversive history and a theologically uncertain
present, and refracted through the prism of folklore and fairy
faith. A simple application of this syndrome to Anglo-Irish
guilt at living in Big Houses on the proceeds of dispossession is
not a sufficient analysis for a complex intellectual and cultural
phenomenon. But this pattern of thought is highly relevant in
understanding Irish Protestant consciousness among a declining
elite in a post-evangelical world.

Irish fictions from the 1850s to the 1880s strikingly reflect this,
notably in the cases of Le Fanu and the Wildes. The connections to Carleton, Emily Lawless, and other writers on the fringe
of this might be explored: Carleton is a particularly interesting
instance, as a convert to Protestantism from a Catholic peasant

FIGURE 39 William Carleton
by John Slattery

background, which allowed him an aggressive claim on authenticity. His Protestantism damned him in the eyes of later nationalist commentators, but provides an enlightening prism through
which to view the imagery of horror in novels such as *Valentine
M'Clutchy* (1845) or *The Squanders of Castle Squander* (1852). The
bleakness of Carleton's view no less than his demonization of
Catholicism brings him closer to the world of the *DUM* writers like Le Fanu; the effects of evangelicalism, and a taste for
prophecy, lie at the heart of his work.[42] *Castle Squander*, while
nodding back to *Castle Rackrent*, invokes Dante and *Frankenstein*.
When the young Yeats tried to define a canon of Irish writers
at the end of the nineteenth century, Carleton featured large—
ostensibly as the social historian of peasant Ireland. But there are
aspects of his work which link him to the more *outré* tradition

of the Gothic and the supernatural, which continued to project through the Irish Protestant imagination, and would reach some kind of apotheosis in Yeats himself.

The esoteric and supernatural interests which wind through Yeats's work have been derided as a subject for research by Auden, Eliot, and less distinguished critics. They were also targeted by F. R. Leavis in his 1967 Clark Lectures, where he attacked the way that Yeats's work had become the focus of 'a cult and an industry'. Leavis denounced this cult for

> ...taking Yeats's lifelong addiction to the occult and the esoteric, together with the schematisms and the symbolical elaborations that were its product, with the kind of seriousness that prescribes earnest study of these last—prescribes it as necessary to the appreciation of Yeats's poetry. But it is not.[43]

'Which isn't', he added cattily, 'the worst that can be said.' What he thought was the worst that could be said about Yeats and his admirers may be left to the imagination. But Leavis's belief that studying Yeats's supernatural interests does not enhance an understanding of his poetry is demonstrably false, as the work of a generation of brilliant critics has shown. And it is even further illuminated when seen as a formation that evolves out of a powerful cultural background, affecting a wide variety of Irish Protestants throughout the nineteenth century, presenting itself through varied forms of supernatural writing—folktales, fairy-lore, Swedenborgian exegesis, stories of demonic possession, and all the rest.

Lord Dunsany's *The Curse of the Wise Woman*, with which we began, nodded at this tradition when it was published in 1933: set in the kind of haunted Big House which dominates the genre, and invoking a world of threat and the resources of the supernatural. Five years after its appearance came an even more striking instance, with Yeats's play *Purgatory*. It is one of his very last works and one of his best plays. An old man, a boy, a half-ruined Big House; an inherited past; a ghostly re-enactment, a parallel world where ancient crimes and curses are constantly relived; a work written, as Yeats himself said, to encapsulate all he thought about this world and the next.[44] The political and eugenic echoes are both worrying and destabilizing. The play has been seen as prefiguring Beckett but it also echoes an equally resonant poem of Yeats's late flowering which was published a few years before: 'The Curse of Cromwell'. The poem gives a voice to a wandering Irish beggar-poet, the victim of invasion, plantation, conquest. The theme is lost Big Houses, though it is not the voice of the Ascendancy we hear but of the native gentry whom their ancestors dispossessed. The last verse, however, invokes the world of *Purgatory*, fairy visions, and the hells which lie all too accessibly around us:

> I came on a great house in the middle of the night,
> Its open lighted doorway and its windows all alight,
> And all my friends were there and made me welcome too;
> But I woke in an old ruin that the winds howled through;
> And when I pay attention I must out and walk
> Among the dogs and horses that understand my talk.
> > *O what of that, O what of that,*
> > *What is there left to say?*

NO. 8 (NEW SERIES) AUGUST 1937.

A BROADSIDE

EDITORS: DOROTHY WELLESLEY, AND W. B. YEATS.
PUBLISHED MONTHLY AT THE CUALA PRESS, ONE HUNDRED
AND THIRTY THREE LOWER BAGGOT STREET, DUBLIN.

THE CURSE OF CROMWELL

You ask what I have found, and far and wide I go,
Nothing but Cromwell's house and Cromwell's murderous crew,
The lovers and the dancers are beaten into the clay,
And the tall men and the swordsmen and the horsemen where are they?
And there is an old beggar wandering in his pride,
His fathers served their fathers before Christ was crucified.

O what of that, O what of that
What is there left to say?

300 copies only.

FIGURE 40 W. B. Yeats's 'The Curse of Cromwell', illustrated by Jack Yeats for the *Broadside* series printed by Cuala Press, 1937

What is left to say is that, to the end of his life, Yeats was re-creating an Irish landscape haunted by history; and that in this he continued to draw on sources in which he had been immersed during his apprenticeship. These involved his readings in Irish folk and fairy lore as well as more ostensibly sophisticated researches into occult and esoteric traditions. They also reflected the world of the insecurely held Big House, which recurred in the folk-memories of his own family, as with so many Irish Protestant families. *Purgatory* came less than a year before his death, but it can serve to remind us that his beginnings and endings circle around into a dramatically satisfying, if in some ways ominous, pattern. It might also remind us that a rich mix of Platonic (or Swedenborgian) correspondences, access to otherworldly phenomena, political uncertainty, and inherited authority surrounded him, as other Irish Protestant writers, from his youth. It was the air he breathed. 'I have not found my tradition in the Catholic Church,' he wrote in 1917, 'but where the tradition is, as I believe, more universal and more ancient.'[45] If he recycled this tradition in unique and wonderful ways, he should nonetheless be seen as the product of a culture which deserves more stringent examination than it usually receives.

4

Oisin Comes Home: Yeats as Inheritor

'Influence', Richard Ellmann has written, 'is a term which conceals and mitigates the guilty acquisitiveness of talent. That writers flow into each other like waves, gently rather than tidally, is one of those decorous myths we impose upon a high-handed, even brutal procedure. The behaviour, while not invariably marked by bad temper, is less polite. Writers move upon other writers not as genial successors but as violent expropriators, knocking down established boundaries to seize by the force of youth, or of age, what they require. They do not borrow, they override.'[1] Ellmann was thinking of Yeats's interactions with his contemporaries; but the same provocative judgements might stand for Yeats's relations to his predecessors.

Yeats's less talented peers sensed early on the high-handedness and acquisitiveness that accompanied genius. In mid 1880s Dublin, Stephen Gwynn—the literary man-about-town and future politician whose strictures on the politicization of Irish nineteenth-century writing opened this book—frequented a group called the Contemporary Club in Dublin. This organization was also attended by the portrait painter John Butler Yeats and his twenty-year-old son, William Butler Yeats. 'Some of us were recognized as counting for something and likely to count for more,' Gwynn recalled much later. 'But every one of us was convinced that Yeats was going to be a better poet than we had yet seen in Ireland; and the significant fact is that this was not out of personal liking.'[2]

Equally significant, perhaps, was the fact that the Contemporary Club was part of a literary movement in the 1880s that included revived Young Ireland reading societies, deliberately trying to reinvigorate the ideas of national literature conjured up by Gavan Duffy, Davis, and others forty years before. The idea of 'revival' was in the air a decade before the name was bestowed on the movement headed by a now-famous Yeats in the 1890s. The *Irish Fireside*, a popular weekly, started a series of historical and biographical articles in mid 1885, in conscious emulation of the *Nation*; in January 1886 it produced a 'Great Irish Revival Number', hailing the resurgence of national literature, language, and music.[3] The *Irish Fireside* in October 1886 published not only Katharine Tynan's call to bring back 'to Irish homes and hearts Mangan and Ferguson, Davis and Duffy', but, a week later, the first surviving piece of published prose by her friend W. B. Yeats—an article on Samuel Ferguson.[4]

The Contemporary Club was equally conscious of precedents and inheritances from the era of Young Ireland, largely because one of its moving spirits was the old Fenian John O'Leary. O'Leary, who had been imprisoned and exiled for advanced-nationalist activity, was an omnivorous reader, book collector, and occasional writer:

FIGURE 41 John O'Leary by
J. B. Yeats, 1887

for the young Yeats he acted as mentor, inspiration, and link to
various Irish traditions not readily accessible to someone of his
protégé's background. It might nonetheless be remembered that
O'Leary was also a Trinity College graduate, a minor landlord,
and was variously described by Douglas Hyde as a 'Tory' and by
Michael Davitt as a 'social shoneen' (in other words, an aspira-
tional and Anglicized bourgeois).[5] This would not have disquali-
fied him from the Contemporary Club, which itself had strong
Trinity College associations; the reconciliation of Protestants to
nationalism was central to its ethos. This, too, looked back to
the 1830s and 1840s, in conscious emulation of the traditions of
Butt and—briefly—Ferguson. In parallel with such movements,
Yeats and his contemporaries were also drawn to the study of
the occult and supernatural, with its own nationalizing angle: he

discovered Theosophy and Eastern mysticism, as well as fairy-lore, in 1880s Dublin, not 1890s London.[6] The 1880s were, in their way, a time of ferment and political expectation in the Irish capital, like the 1840s: ending, like the earlier decade, in catastrophe, with the shattering fall and death of Parnell. It is also the period when Yeats absorbed many of the influences which enabled his emergence as a national poet, signalled by the landmark volume of *Poems* in 1895, just after he turned thirty.[7] The groundwork had been laid.

By the time of that volume, Yeats was well on his way to polishing and integrating his work into a consciously conceived whole, which involved expunging many of the inheritances of Victorian Romanticism. Nonetheless, the literary influences that he was formally jettisoning include his very earliest conditioning: the books which were read to him as a child, and which supplied phrases and incidents that would lie in the seedbed of his imagination for the rest of his life. Walter Scott is just one such; the first books read to the young Yeatses included Scott's three great novels *Old Mortality*, *The Antiquary*, and *Redgauntlet*, as well as *The Lay of the Last Minstrel*—which Yeats himself, half a century later, would read to his own children.[8] The concept 'anxiety of influence' has a special resonance for Yeats, and Scott (like Tennyson and Swinburne) is someone who generally merits dismissal in Yeats's critical commentaries; but, as with these others, this should make us slightly suspicious. The evasions of Yeats's autobiographical writings are as significant as the inclusions, and this applies to his discussion of literary influence as to other areas. From very early on, Yeats was determined to create a literary pedigree for himself, and this meant rejecting unsuitable avatars.

It also nvolved, at the outset of his career, adopting a deceptive simplicity of language which would suggest a connection to the authenticity of the peasantry, or 'country people'—later, of course, to be traded in for a hieratic complexity. As John Frayne has put it, 'he did not wait for scholars to unearth a long line of bards stretching back to Ossian—he created his pedigree... Certain pretenders had to be exposed, some contemporary claimants had to be rejected, and as Yeats developed his style from peasant simplicity to aristocratic obscurity the patents of nobility were changed continually.'[9] The great autodidact was going to emerge as the great original.

However, this underestimates his recognition of a tradition that had gone before—however ambivalently he judged it. His earliest work relied on a grounding in nineteenth-century Romantic history and fiction, folklore collections, fairylore, Young Ireland rhetoric (supplied from O'Leary's library), Swedenborgian mysticism, the inheritance of a haunted history, and translated legends and sagas. All that came before the rewritten *Poems* of 1895— *The Wanderings of Oisin* (1889), *The Countess Kathleen and Various Legends and Lyrics* (1892), *The Celtic Twilight* (1893)—would simply not have been possible without them. This is borne out by the fact that these apprenticeship years are also a time of deliberate self-education in the neglected literary texts of the early years of the Union. Well into the 1890s, the process of creating a literary self at the same time as creating a canon of Irish literature was at the centre of Yeats's project, and this was closely bound in with the agenda of political nationalism; towards the end of that decade, his priorities underwent a decisive shift in both spheres. He had spent the immediately preceding period as inheritor and investigator of a rich and varied tradition that had gone before. Yeats's debt to Shelleyan Romanticism and Orientalism has been closely prospected by George Bornstein, and his readings in Irish folklore illuminated by Mary Helen Thuente, Warwick Gould, and Deirdre Toomey; otherwise, apart from the pioneering work of Phillip L. Marcus forty years ago and some recent suggestive comments by Matthew Campbell, there is curiously little commentary on the complex of inherited influences that surrounded him as he began to write and find his voice.[10] That his voice was, at this stage, self-consciously political as well as literary makes the process all the more interesting, and all the more complex.

Here, Yeats's background is important (as any member of the Contemporary Club would have recognized at once): Irish Protestant, a mixture of bourgeois and *déclassé*, with clerics and small landowners on the Yeats side, businessmen and provincial worthies among his mother's family, the Pollexfens. By his early twenties he was used to living, insecurely, between Dublin, London, and Sligo; not destined for Trinity College but for art college; used to the wide-ranging conversation of his father's studio and the wide resources of John and Ellen O'Leary's library but essentially self-educated from his own readings in the British Museum and (later) the National Library of Ireland. They were both institutions to which, like Shaw, he paid frequent tribute later in life. These were the locations where he would have found, for instance, the *Transactions of the Ossianic Society*,[11] which gave him the dialogue between Oisin (or Ossian) and Saint Patrick which lies behind his epic poem *The Wanderings of Oisin*. He began working on it aged twenty—the age when, he was fond of repeating, Napoleon said that a person's character and interests were fixed for life. 'I am persuaded that our intellects at twenty contain all the truths we shall ever find,' he wrote much later, 'but as yet we do not know truths that belong to us from opinions caught up in casual irritation or momentary fantasy.'[12] This picks up one echo from the earlier age of Literary Romanticism. And in 1886, aged twenty-one, he would sound another, with his first critique of the Irish literary tradition: an extended treatment of, and tribute to, Samuel Ferguson, claimed by Yeats as the greatest Irish poet because the most 'Celtic'—and also, implicitly and explicitly, the most 'Homeric'. (Or perhaps Ossianic.)

Epic poetry seemed to the apprentice Yeats in the mid 1880s to represent the unity of life, against the fracture and dissonance of modernity: an interpretation which would have been very familiar to his early-nineteenth-century Romantic predecessors and which brings us back to the quarrels over Ossian and the desire for the simplicity and even the 'savagery' of a sincere and harmonious prelapsarian universe. Ferguson, in Yeats's youthful view, demonstrated the heroic poet's ability to sweep his fingers over the strings of the lute that represented man's whole nature, and rouse him to action. What Yeats got out of Ferguson's synthetic-epical poetry was the impact of characters embedded in their environment—as opposed to the modern cult of character for its own sake. (These are the antagonisms which he would shortly try to explore in his own epic, *The Wanderings of Oisin*.) Ferguson is a vital figure for Yeats's apprenticeship, first because of the sources which Ferguson had plundered for *his* epics: the story behind *Congal*, of a Gaelic king insulted by being offered the wrong kind of food at a feast and taking his revenge, would re-emerge in Yeats's own late play *The Herne's Egg*, at a time when he was reverting to ballad and Gaelic legend. But early on he was most clearly influenced by Ferguson's use of Gaelic metres and a certain deceptive simplicity of language, particularly apparent in Ferguson's translations, such as 'Cashel of Munster':

> I'd wed you without herds, without money, or rich array,
> And I'd wed you on a dewy morning at day-dawn grey;
> My bitter woe it is, love, that we are not far away
> In Cashel town, though the bare deal board were our
>   marriage bed this day![13]

For his early love-lyrics, Yeats discovered a language similarly vocative, exclamatory, and incantatory:

> I would that we were, my beloved, white birds on the foam
>   of the sea!
> We tire of the flame of the meteor, before it can fade and flee;
> And the flame of the blue star of twilight, hung low on the
>   rim of the sky,
> Has awaked in our hearts, my beloved, a sadness that
>   may not die.[14]

Significantly, Yeats's second and more substantial article on Ferguson was published in the *Dublin University Review*. This magazine was a deliberate attempt to revive the spirit and ethos of the old *DUM*, as part of a Protestant-nationalist initiative arising among a group of Trinity College mavericks (overlapping closely with the Contemporary Club). It also had a distinct cult of Thomas Davis, another illustrious predecessor. Behind its title page of Celtic interlace, the *DUR* featured articles by 'A Protestant Nationalist' (probably C. H. Oldham) and another Trinity academic F. J. Gregg, proclaiming himself 'a Presbyterian nationalist'; Mohini Chatterjee's 'The Common Sense of Theosophy' appeared cheek by jowl with a reprint of Thomas Davis's 'Chronology of Ireland' and Yeats's early poems (later ruthlessly expelled from the canon).[15] This was the logical scenario for a reappraisal of Ferguson, stressing his Irish and national credentials. Ferguson's stately, grave, elaborately simple language showed Yeats a way into Anglo-Irish speech that offered an alternative to the parodies of Lever and Lover.[16] In his critique of Ferguson's work, moreover, Yeats was acutely conscious of the circumstances of his subject's life, engaging fully with the society in which Ferguson was embedded. The deliberate decision to advance Ferguson as part of the 'Revival' project from 1885 is a clear reminder that the canonical 'Revival'

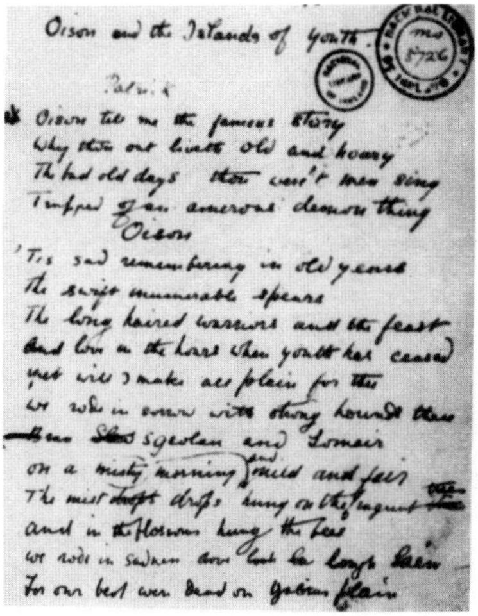
Oisin and the Islands of Youth
Patrick
Oisin tell me the famous story
Oisin
'Tis sad remembering in old years
The long haired warriors and the feast
And in the flowers hung the bees
For our best were dead on Gabra's plain

FIGURE 42 Early manuscript draft of *The Wanderings of Oisin* by W. B. Yeats of the *fin de siècle* did not look back to Gaelic origins only; it had its unacknowledged early-Victorian inspirations too.

In the years just after his lengthy appreciation of Ferguson, Yeats was working on his own Fergusonian epic poem, *The Wanderings of Oisin*, for which he would search out translations of medieval Irish texts such as the Book of Leinster, published in the 1850s by the Ossianic Society, and those produced by the Royal Irish Academy and other learned societies. The Irish need to combat Macpherson was still sharply felt: Hyde claimed that at this time he found people on Achill Island who could recite tales straight from Ossian.[17] And Yeats's sources were impeccably Irish. Notably, he adopted the framework of the *Agallamh na Seanórach*, or *Dialogue of the Old Men*, a reconstituted imaginary conversation between Saint Patrick, Oisin, son of the Fianna leader Fionn Mac Cumhaill, and another member of the Fianna. This framing device may have originally derived from a Christianizing process at the hands of a monastic scribe, but in the originals it is also used to express robustly anticlerical views. The Saint Patrick-versus-Oisin argument, as mentioned in the last chapter, crops up in fairylore, too; and it also recurs in many versions of medieval stories and poems. By the early nineteenth century it was a well-established trope, referred to casually in novels like Sydney Owenson's *The O'Briens and the O'Flahertys*. Yeats adapted a popularized eighteenth-century version attributed to the poet Michael Comyn, in order to to suggest the struggle between the worlds of contemplation and action and, implicitly, between acceptance of the status quo and revolutionary action—as well as the tension between intellectualism and sensuality. Half a century later, Yeats would decide that *The Wanderings of Oisin*, started in early

1886 when he was twenty, already summed up the themes which he was still addressing at the end of his career: 'the swords man throughout repudiates the saint, but not without vacilation [*sic*]—Is that perhaps the sole theme—Usheen & Patrick...'[18] Certainly Oisin's travels through enchanted islands, led on by a fairy temptress, suggest private allegories; but Oisin's refusal of Saint Patrick at the end, and his declared commitment to the lost but inspirational world of the Fenians (not the Fianna), would not have been misread by John O'Leary.[19]

This declares Yeats's own politics, which were nationalist, with a strong sense of making amends for his own ancestry; no one in his Sligo youth had recited to him ancient Irish sagas, as he lamented much later.[20] Politically, for the young Yeats, Ferguson represented the way Unionist, Protestant, 'respectable' Ireland had turned its back on nationalism. When, a few years later, Yeats had occasion to review Lady Ferguson's tribute-biography to her late husband, he was able to clarify this, with many swipes at the Trinity-bourgeois culture from whose nets his own father had flown. Ferguson had, by contrast, embraced it and (in Yeats's view) by so doing inhibited his own early genius. But the veteran translator and poet, formed by the *DUM* circle of the 1830s, remained a kind of Platonic nationalist—endorsed, indeed, by John O'Leary as having done more for Irish cultural identity than the old Fenian himself. For someone in Yeats's position, this was a vital steer, and lies behind Ferguson's inclusion in a celebrated triumvirate of influences in Yeats's 1892 manifesto 'To Ireland in the Coming Times'. This repeated and endorsed his friend Tynan's invocation of inspirational poets in the age of Young Ireland.

> *Nor may I less be counted one*
> *With Davis, Mangan, Ferguson,*
> *Because to him who ponders well*
> *My rhymes more than their rhyming tell*
> *Of the dim wisdoms old and deep*
> *That God gives unto man in sleep.*[21]

Those 'dim wisdoms', as we have seen, were not summoned up by Yeats alone; they link him back to a long Irish tradition. However, the emphasis here falls on his wish to claim Davis and Mangan, no less than Ferguson. Yeats's relationship with the poetry and traditions of Young Ireland is central to his process of self-fashioning in his early twenties. It is a far more complex story than a simple rejection of their mechanical versification in favour of a truly Irish (or even 'Celtic') literary form—though that is how some later critics, following Yeats's own later simplifications, have seen it. Writing about Ferguson, Protestant and Unionist though he was, allowed the young Yeats to differentiate himself and invoke the world he was discovering through the Contemporary Club and John O'Leary:

I do not appeal to the professorial classes, who, in Ireland, at least, appear at no time to have thought of the affairs of the country till they at first feared for their emolument—nor do I appeal to the shoddy society of 'West Britonism'—but to those young men clustered here and there throughout our land, whom the emotion of patriotism has lifted into that world of selfless passion in which heroic deeds are possible and heroic poetry credible.[22]

This declared a nationalist agenda by invoking the contemporary literary Young Ireland societies which Yeats would in a few years try to build into a broad-front literary movement; it anticipates his own 'heroic' poem which he would work upon for the next two years; and it looks back (inspired by a younger Ferguson) to the 1830s world of the *DUM* (out of whose back numbers Yeats would shortly be extracting literary material for inclusion in his anthologies).

O'Leary had used the Young Ireland societies as a springboard into cultural agitation on his return to Dublin in 1885, when he delivered the widely acclaimed speech 'Young Ireland: The Old and the New'.[23] This argued—*inter alia*—for a pluralist nationalism, embracing various approaches to independence. Though their Fenian origins became diluted from the mid 1880s, the Young Ireland societies had been in existence since 1881, and Matthew Kelly has convincingly argued that they provided 'the organisational crucible of the literary revival and the cultural nationalism of the *fin de siècle*'—much as Yeats himself suggested in the introduction to his anthology *Representative Irish Tales* ten years later.[24] The societies pressed for commemorative activities and the raising of monuments to national heroes, among whom Davis and Mangan figured large—a campaign strongly supported by Oldham in the *DUR*. Their meetings took place in York Street, off Stephen's Green; the same street housed John Butler Yeats's studio. Yeats would later instance the conversation in that studio as one of his key educational influences; he might have added the discussions in the neighbouring rooms of the Young Ireland Society, which revolved around recognizing the achievements and relevance of the 'men of '48'.

At the same time, the 1840s Young Ireland movement provides yet another instance of Yeats's anxiety about influence. From

this vital period of his apprenticeship, through his readings in
O'Leary's library, he was acutely conscious of the inspirational
influence of Thomas Davis on Irish national literature, especially
through Gavan Duffy's *Ballad Poetry of Ireland* (the very book
Duffy gave to Jane Carlyle); since it also included many Ferguson
poems, it might be seen as a sort of sacred book for the young
Yeats. But he became increasingly conscious through the 1890s
that the Davisite style of balladry was uncomfortably near dog-
gerel, and that his own literary mission was to move things to a
more demanding plane. The way that Wallis described the *Nation*
poets setting themselves to create utilitarian verse would have
made him wince. Hence his critical remarks about Davis in his
introduction to *A Book of Irish Verse* (1895). By 1899 he was annoy-
ing colleagues in the Irish Literary Society by describing Davis's
'Battle of Fontenoy' as 'a clever imitation of Macaulay...mere
journalistic and rhetorical poetry', arousing a chorus of disagreement and giving A. P. Graves (no nationalist) the opportunity
for a catty put-down: 'Davis had not, perhaps, the leisure which
Mr Yeats enjoys to polish his golden numbers.'[25]

Yet if Yeats was to carve himself a place in nationalist politics and a national literary tradition, Davis was a vital figure in
the pantheon: like Yeats, he was a middle-class Protestant who
had somehow achieved authenticity and whose national credentials were unimpeachable, but who had preached reconciliation
and pluralism. In 1897 Yeats praised Young Ireland for teaching
'fervour and labour and religious toleration'[26]—principles which
remained his bedrock. This is the Davis to whom Yeats would
recur at several key junctures of his later life—notably when he
wrote his great farewell to the simplicities of national piety in

1909, the essay 'J. M. Synge and the Ireland of his Time'. There, he applauded Davis's 'moral simplicity', but made it clear that this negated an achieved style or artistic originality. Later still, when he debated against Patrick Pearse during the Davis centenary in 1914, he used the occasion to formally recant his overreaction against Davis's poetry in his younger days and to warmly praise (for instance) Davis's 'Lament for Owen Roe O'Neill'; the whole speech, in fact, reveals a close acquaintance with Davis's life-story as well as with his work.[27] Shortly before, in similar mood, he had invoked a Davis poem, 'The Green above the Red', in his excoriating denunciation of small-minded Irish piety, 'September 1913', when he declared 'Romantic Ireland's dead and gone, / It's with O'Leary in the grave'.[28]

By then, the development and ownership of the Irish Literary Revival had already become a subject for historians. The first book on the subject, by W. P. Ryan, appeared in 1894, and controversy about the origins of the phenomenon has continued from that day to this. But it seems increasingly clear that its seeds lie in the literary societies of the mid 1880s, when the Young Ireland ethos was revived, rather than in the fallout following Parnell's death six years later. This latter juncture was, however, the moment when Davis and the literary culture of Young Ireland became an electric issue between Yeats and none other than one of the original Young Irelanders—the aged Charles Gavan Duffy.

In the early 1890s the young poet-critic and the elder statesman came to blows over the content of a revived Library of Ireland: a series of key texts, to be published under the auspices of the Irish Literary Society. The extraordinary trajectory of Duffy's career has already been indicated. In 1892, recently retired and living between Nice and London, he saw a potential route back into Irish cultural politics at a vital moment. Duffy wanted to republish the canonical texts of his long-ago Young Ireland contemporaries; Yeats wanted not only to advance his own friends but to infiltrate the more abrasive politics of Parnellism after the split in the Irish Parliamentary Party, which effectively meant neo-Fenianism. And Duffy, whose nationalism was by now emphatically moderate and imperial in orientation, supported the anti-Parnellite side. The quarrel over the contents of the Library of Ireland was also a quarrel over the political agenda for the coming generation.

This is not how Yeats would remember it later, in his *Autobiographies*; like Duffy himself, he knew the importance of capturing the record through memoirs. By the time he sat down to rewrite history in the early 1920s, Yeats would claim that his priorities had been uncompromisingly artistic, while Duffy's were corruptly political.

When we remember Duffy in his neo-Carlylean youth as the *Nation*'s editor, it is slightly shocking to turn to Yeats's recollection of their tussles over the National Literary Society and the Library of Ireland nearly half a century later:

> Sir Charles Gavan Duffy arrived. He brought with him much manuscript, the private letters of a Young Ireland poetess, a dry but informing unpublished historical essay by Davis, and an unpublished novel by William Carleton, into the middle of which he had dropped a hot coal, so that nothing remained but the borders of every page. He hired a young man to read him, after dinner, Carlyle's *Heroes and Hero-Worship,* and before

dinner was gracious to all our men of authority and especially
to our Harps and Pepperpots [i.e., pietistic nationalist politi-
cians]. Taylor compared him to Odysseus returning to Ithaca,
and every newspaper published his biography. He was a white-
haired old man, who had written the standard history of Young
Ireland, had emigrated to Australia, had been the first Australian Federalist, and later Prime Minister, but, in all his writings,
in which there is so much honesty, so little rancour, there is not
one sentence which has any meaning when separated from its
place in argument or narrative, not one distinguished because
of its thought or music. One imagined his youth in some gaunt
little Irish town, where no building or custom is revered for its
antiquity; and there speaking a language where no word, even
in solitude, is ever spoken slowly and carefully because of emo-
tional implication; and of his manhood of practical politics, of
the dirty piece of orange-peel in the corner of the stairs as one
climbs up to some newspaper office; of public meetings where
it would be treacherous amid so much geniality to speak or
even to think of anything that might cause a moment's mis-
understanding in one's own party. No argument of mine was
intelligible to him...[29]

That piece of orange-peel is pure genius, but the unfairness of
the whole thing is devastating: Duffy's dynamic cultural agenda
in the 1840s, his founding of the *Nation*, his close friendship with
Carlyle, are either ignored or belittled into satire. We are dealing with the authentically Olympian Yeats of the 1920s, and the
Paterian prose conceals multiple elisions and false directions.
You would not guess from this that other young literary activ-
ists of the time, like Douglas Hyde, found Duffy practical, well
connected, and efficient (so much so that he swiftly captured the
reins of the publishing company behind the venture, and smartly

cut Yeats out of the Library by accusing him of fomenting 'sectional interests'). Nor does Yeats's recollection indicate that at the time being spoken of, he was himself, at twenty-seven, already a veteran of those unswept staircases leading up to newspaper offices. Through such places, he was broadcasting an extraordinary range of articles, criticism, and poems, and he would himself shortly emerge as a featured public speaker at nationalist public meetings in the Fenian interest.[30] But it is a vivid illustration of the ways in which the past history of Irish political literature caught up with the present, in the 1880s and 1890s, and how implicated Yeats was in the process.

The section of his *Autobiographies* called 'Ireland after Parnell' is a marvellous evocation of the age, but is implicitly viewed through the prism of the intervening Irish Revolution of 1916–22. By the time of the first draft of his memoirs, Yeats had moved far away from Young Ireland. 'Young Irelandism, because a condescension, a conscious simplification, could only perish or create a tyranny.'[31] But this is not how he had felt in the 1880s and early 1890s. To recapture Yeats's position at the actual time requires stripping off layers of fabulous polish applied to his memoirs; the echoes and inspiration of Young Ireland which he omits or denies in his *Autobiographies* meant far more to him at the time. This is confirmed by his contemporary writings—perhaps most vividly by poems which he excluded from his canon, or was wise enough to leave unpublished.

> This song unto all who would gather together and hold
>   Brother by brother;
> A watch and award by the watch-fire of Eri, our old
>   And long-weeping mother.

This song unto all who would stand by the fire of her hope,
    And droop not nor slumber;
But keep up the high and the mirthful proud courage to cope
      With wrongs beyond number.

This song unto all who would gather and help yet once more
      Eri, our mother;
And do nought that would anger the famous and great gone before
      Brother by brother.[32]

Speranza and Thomas Davis lurk in the background, for better or worse. Nor was Davis the only Young Irelander to maintain an important place in Yeats's imagination, at least up to the great shift in his consciousness that begins around 1916. John Mitchel's *Jail Journal* and *The Last Conquest of Ireland (Perhaps)* echo through Yeats's work: in that same passage of his *Autobiographies* where he traduces Gavan Duffy, he refers to Mitchel as 'the only Young Irelander who had music and personality, though rancorous and devil-possessed'. Mitchel's violence and passion struck clanging chords that Yeats returned to in his poems of the 1930s, notably 'Under Ben Bulben'. In the period of his apprenticeship, however, it was the doomed poet James Clarence Mangan who meant most to him and whom he hailed as 'strange, exotic, different' (thus buying into Mangan's cult of himself, from which later critics have tried to disentangle him). Mangan's unhappy life struck a strong echo in Yeats's youthful consciousness, at a time of particular poverty and insecurity—vividly illustrated by his father's image of him as a deranged Gaelic king from one of his early poems, 'The Madness of King Goll'. More importantly, the young Yeats acutely noted the astonishing and original poetic

FIGURE 43 *King Goll*
by J. B. Yeats, using
W. B. Yeats as a model, 1887

effects which Mangan was capable of, in poems like 'Siberia' as well as 'My Dark Rosaleen'. He also absorbed—as he had from Ferguson—the manner in which Mangan, working through translations, utilized the arresting metres of Gaelic poetry, such as the ending of a line on three equally stressed beats—a form used to great effect in 'The Lake Isle of Innisfree', written at this very time.

His discovery of the range and variety of Mangan's work serves as a reminder that in the late 1880s and early 1890s, when he had moved to London, he was prospecting through back numbers of the Irish periodicals of the early nineteenth century, and persuading friends to make transcriptions out of, for instance, the *DUM*. This was in the cause of putting together anthologies, which for him was a vital process of self-education—notably where folklore was concerned. But it also led him back to the fiction of the age of Edgeworth, Maturin, and the Banims. He would later give credit to the nineteenth-century Irish novelists for supplying a large part of his literary education. He wrote uneasily but with sharp perception about *Castle Rackrent* (which was in some ways a bit too close to home, or at least to the home he was detaching himself from); he formed a considerable respect for the Banim brothers; but, most potently, he discovered Carleton, whose work Yeats not only anthologized in his first collection, *Fairy and Folk Tales of the Irish Peasantry* (1888), but collected in two other forgotten early anthologies, *Stories from Carleton* (1889) and *Representative Irish Tales* (1891). It was Carleton who inspired one of Yeats's most striking images, when he described Carleton's treatment of country people's lives as a sort of 'fiery shorthand', like children waving a lighted stick through the dark night air.

Yeats's relationship to Carleton was—as with his approach to Davis—sensitive: for Carleton was widely seen by Irish nationalist readers as an apostate, having converted to Protestantism. In a detailed and rather serpentine critique, Yeats proved to his own satisfaction that Carleton had actually stayed, so to speak, Platonically Catholic.[33] His other rationalization for reading Carleton was that this writer alone presented an authentic social history of the Irish peasantry—their beliefs, prejudices, strengths, and weaknesses—while never stooping to the stereotyping and condescension of Lever or Lover. This critique would be reproduced in the next few years by critics such as Maurice Egan and Stephen Gwynn.[34] Yeats would also present his own anthology

Representative Irish Tales as 'a kind of social history', declaring a very specific function for nineteenth-century Irish fiction.[35] Even more gratifyingly, Carleton's links to the world of supernatural belief, alternatives to Catholic magic, and the aesthetic of horror, supplied him with an additional voltage for Yeats. The genuine excitement with which Yeats in the 1880s approached the neglected world of Irish writing in the early nineteenth century would be replaced after the turn of the century by his investigations in other spheres. These included English dramatists and poets of the sixteenth and seventeenth centuries, and an astonishing variety of occult philosophers. He would also by then have determined on an approach to Irish culture that would make essentially Irish modes and traditions into something new and strange, in the manner of J. M. Synge. But his determined categorization of Irish nineteenth-century fiction in the 1880s and 1890s has imposed restrictions and assumptions on the genre which have inhibited interpretation ever since.[36] Here and elsewhere, Yeats's cultural importance and influence as a highly political literary critic has yet to receive its due. So has the extent to which his early mentors shaped his own first writings.

This reading shaped his own essays at fiction in the 1880s and 1890s, most of it remaining unpublished: the fact that *John Sherman* was his only published novel (or novella) should not let us ignore *The Speckled Bird*, on which he slaved for much of the 1890s, though it remained unfinished and was never published in his lifetime. And both texts, in their different ways, closely reflect his reading of Irish nineteenth-century novelists. The realistic depiction of Irish provincial life to be found in the Banims or Griffin, anthologized by Yeats, clearly shapes *John Sherman*:

he himself confirmed this, claiming to Katharine Tynan that it was 'as much an Irish novel as anything by Banim or Griffen [*sic*]'.[37] Less obviously, the world of the early-nineteenth-century national tale is conjured up by *The Speckled Bird*, with its haunted Big Houses in a lonely Western landscape, and a narrative invoking Jacobitism, Rosicrucianism, secret societies, French connections, and ancient aristocracies. The journey to the Gaelic West, home of ancient aristocracy and autochthonous values, is easily familiar to us from Owenson, Edgeworth, Maturin, and others, and echoes of *The O'Briens and the O'Flahertys* resonate. Yeats's early short story *Dhoya*, published with *John Sherman*, is also modelled closely on his reading of folktales retold by Croker and Carleton. The derivation and inspiration of his more accomplished occult short stories gathered in the 1890s as *The Secret Rose* also present intriguing Irish inheritances, as their modern editors have consummately shown.

Nor is the effect on the young Yeats of his obscure Irish literary predecessors to be found only in his anthologies and his own attempts at fiction. Just as vividly, his apprenticeship was marked out by aggressive attempts to construct an official canon of acceptable models in Irish literature that would afforce the politics of the day. The compilation *Representative Irish Tales* can be seen as one salvo in this battle; in the introduction, written at the height of the Parnell split, he declared, 'We are preparing likely enough for a new Irish literary movement—like that of '48—that will show itself at the first lull in this storm of politics.'[38] There were several signs that this was happening, notably in the columns of *United Ireland*.[39] He was equally single-minded in his campaign to dictate the contents of the revived Library of

Ireland and the National Publishing Company, where he lost out to Duffy, and in his attempts to ignite a controversy over a list of 'Best Irish Books'. For the Library of Ireland in 1892 he had hoped to include Ossianic literature, as well as Mitchel and some of *The Spirit of the Nation* volume: this was part of his attempt to beat Duffy at his own game, and to raise against him the more radical spirit of Mitchel.[40] Three years later he was far more specific, and suggestive, when he instigated a controversy over the 'Best Irish Books'[41]—a campaign coinciding with his heavyweight articles in the Bookman on 'Irish National Literature'.

'Lists' were as popular a way of generating newsprint a hundred years ago as they are now. In 1886 Barry O'Brien in the *Freeman's Journal* had started a buzz with an attempt to compile a list of the 'Best Hundred Irish Books', published as an influential pamphlet and arousing many responses. Yeats, still living in Dublin at that stage, clearly paid it close attention. O'Leary had been much involved, passionately denouncing Sydney Owenson and, less expectedly, praising Matthew Arnold on Celtic literature.[42] When Yeats returned to the matter of drawing up a list in 1895, he declared an intention to exclude directly political material—an indication of the way his own interests were tending, but also an attempt to regain the initiative from the Duffy camp. His canonization campaign also was directly influenced by the fact that he had recently been involved in further Oedipal exchanges (via the Dublin *Daily Express*) with Edward Dowden, not only about the claims of Samuel Ferguson as an Irish poet but about the achievements of Yeats's own movement (as it was already coming to be seen).[43]

When Yeats laid down the gauntlet of his own best thirty Irish books in the *Daily Express* of 27 February 1895, they included much that we have already encountered: *Castle Rackrent*, a story and several poems by Ferguson, three books by Carleton, *The Nowlans* by John Banim, Griffin's *The Collegians*, as well as Lever, Lover, Lawless, and Standish O'Grady. He also had to push his own contemporaries, so Hyde and Katharine Tynan appear on the initial list (he was on the point of bringing out yet another anthology, *A Book of Irish Verse*). A long commentary was appended, the controversy gratifyingly spread into other journals, and Yeats extended his list to forty items for a combative article in the *Bookman* the following October. Yet again, the inevitable comparison with Scotland occurs:

> The time has not yet come for Irishmen, as it has for Scotsmen, to carry about with them a subtle national feeling, no matter when, or of what they write, because that feeling has yet to be perfectly elaborated and expounded by men of genius with minds as full of Irish history, scenery and character as the minds of Burns and Scott were full of Scottish history, scenery and character. For a like reason it contains many imperfect books, which seem to me to hide under a mound of melodrama or sheer futility a smouldering and fragrant fire that cannot be had elsewhere in the world.[44]

Yeats's accompanying remarks suggest, however, that he was moving on from the influences of his youth. Writing of Carleton and Banim, he remarks:

> These books can only have been prevented from taking their place as great literature because the literary tradition of Ireland was, when Carleton and Banim wrote, so undeveloped that

a novelist, no matter how great his genius, found no fit convention ready to his hands, and no exacting public to forbid him to
commingle noisy melodrama with his revelations. England can
afford to forget these books, but we cannot, because for all their
imperfections they contain the most remarkable records yet
made of Irish habits and passions.[45]

Thus the main claim to be made for the early-nineteenth-century Irish novel was as social history, not original literature—a
bias and a perspective that would endure among later critics.
This is relevant to a striking observation made later in the same
letter, when he refers to 'the fallacy of our time, which says that
the fountain of art is observation, whereas it is almost wholly
experience. The creations of a great writer are little more than
the moods and passions of his own heart, given surnames and
Christian names, and sent to walk the earth.' These are the kinds
of reflections which implicitly contradict his schematic generalizations about the epic, dramatic, and lyric phases of national
literature succeeding each other—which, as will be seen, he had
categorically advanced less than two years before. But the idea
that art stems from passionate experience rather than abstract
observation may also reflect the reasons why his awkwardly
contrived novel *The Speckled Bird* would never see the light of
day, whereas he was already writing poems which would triumphantly stand the test of time.

Yeats's relationship to his nineteenth-century Irish literary
predecessors at the outset of his career can be clearly established,
and the contradictions which it sometimes embodies reflect a
youthful mind in the course of formation at a hectic time of life.

Equally suggestive is another aspect of his apprenticeship, which also involves the construction of canons and taxonomies and the creation of anthologies and lists. This concerns his *Fairy and Folk Tales of the Irish Peasantry*, put together in a concentrated burst of work in 1888. It repays close attention both for its structure and for the kind of authorities he appealed to. These investigations also brought him back yet again to writers such as Carleton and Ferguson, who supplied legends and stories. In a way, *Fairy and Folk Tales of the Irish Peasantry* led straight on to *Stories from Carleton*, which Yeats published less than a year later, in 1889.[46]

FIGURE 44 Max Beerbohm's cartoon of Yeats presenting George Moore to the Queen of the Fairies, 1904

The type of tales Yeats sought out, and the way he defined them, is also significant, placing him consciously in the tradition of Crofton Croker and the Wildes, though he carefully distinguished his approach from theirs.

Yeats's approach to fairies was highly specific. His involvement in their world was not adequately conveyed in Max Beerbohm's sublime cartoon of a dreamy but socially adept Yeats introducing George Moore to the Queen of the Fairies. He was determined to separate himself from the scientific and anthropological analysts of folktales on the one hand, and those collectors like Hyde on the other, who believed in the fundamental historical origin of the stories. But he nonetheless read widely in the *Folk-Lore Journal* (finding it useless because 'scientific people cannot tell stories') and the *Folk-Lore Record* as well as more general magazines, and rapidly caught up with works by d'Arbois de Jubainville and Ernest Rhys (though the latter's trailblazing Hibbert Lectures were not published until after Yeats's first collection appeared).[47] Like other commentators, Yeats distinguished between fairytales on the one hand, which he interpreted as legends, often attached to a geographical locality, and on the other, folktales, of a more universal and symbolic variety.

The stories which Yeats himself liked most are strongly in the Irish occult tradition, where the dead continue a parallel life with the living. His particular favourite (supplied by Hyde, who later published it in *Leabhar Sgeulaigheachta*) was 'Teig O'Kane and the Corpse'. A tearaway country boy, with an eye for the girls, is disciplined by a fairy troop who fasten a corpse to his shoulders and decree that he must bury it before sunrise: saddled with this terrible burden, he staggers around the countryside, transformed by moonlight, trying to fulfil his task. But when he tries, other corpses erupt from the ground, or rear up in front of him, driving him demented. He succeeds at the end and henceforth leads a reformed life. This story, anticipatory of Máirtín Ó Cadhain's graveyard comedy *Cré na Cille*, was Yeats's emphatic favourite: he included in his list of thirty 'Best Irish Books' and was still referring to it decades later.[48] He does not interpret it anthropologically, or as a metaphorical treatment of the search for sensual experience amid the conventions of everyday rural life. In a similar way, a superstition retailed by Lady Wilde appealed to him in a direct manner: 'If you love in vain, all you have to do is go to a graveyard at midnight, dig up a corpse, and take a strip of skin off it from head to heel, watch until you catch your mistress

FIGURE 45 Augusta Gregory, early 1900s

sleeping and tie it round her waist, and thereafter she will love you forever.'[49] This activity is rather a long way from the antics of Mustardseed and Peaseblossom, but squarely in the tradition of Le Fanu and Carleton.

Yeats's collecting of fairytales just predates his anthologizing the writers of the earlier nineteenth century, and the crash course which he set himself in reading them. But the fairy and folktale immersion would prove the more lasting. By the early twentieth century he could airily refer to having forgotten all about Carleton.[50] But his preoccupation with folktales as representing an ancient 'aristocracy of thought' strengthened and deepened with time, as can be seen from his marvellous essay 'Swedenborg, Mediums, and the Desolate Places', written in 1914 and published as an introduction to Augusta Gregory's *Visions and Beliefs in the West of Ireland* in 1920. His friendship with Gregory from 1896 set him upon a different path from the frantic activities of the previous decade, and marks a caesura in his life. The analysis of the supernatural which Yeats embarked upon at this stage played a vital part in his intellectual and creative progression, whereby folklore became for him a repository of wisdoms that were occult as well as traditional, and are intertwined with his own psychic and supernatural investigations and disciplines. This can be tracked through the supernatural short stories gathered as *The Secret Rose* in 1897. Fairies would give way to ghosts, as Conrad Arensberg's classic anthropological study *The Irish Countryman* remarked in 1937.[51] But for Yeats they had been, in a sense, ghosts all along.

Before then, however, came the work which first aroused the interest of his future Galway collaborator: *The Celtic Twilight* of

FIGURE 46 *The Fairy Greyhound* by Jack
Yeats, for *Irish Fairy Tales*, 1892

1893. In some ways this might be seen simply as a distilled collection of the stories, traditions, and reflections prepared for by his earlier anthologizing. Much of the material had been published by him already. But the tone of the collection is striking, and deliberately his own. What he had learned from earlier compilers and retailers was exactly what to avoid: whimsy, dialect, prosy moralizing. (His earlier anthologizing of, for instance, Crofton Croker had silently omitted or amended these very characteristics.) The illustrations by his brother Jack for yet another compilation (*Irish Fairy Tales*, 1892) beautifully echo the odd matter-of-factness involved when the Otherworld intersects with Irish country life, conjuring up such images as 'a fairy greyhound'. This tone of everyday acceptance was part of Yeats's effort 'to write in an Irish way' (as he believed Ferguson had done). In its initial 1893 version, *The Celtic Twilight* also contained legends rather than folktales. These last were brought in to the expanded version in 1902, illustrating once again the development of his interests and a refinement of approach; in 1902, also, Yeats introduced more directly autobiographical material about his own experiences. Even in the first version, however, the concrete note of locale is combined with a deliberately offhand tone regarding the supernatural. 'Drumcliff and Rosses are choke-full of ghosts. By bog, road, rath, hillside, sea-border they gather in all shapes: headless women, men in armour, shadow hares, fire-tongued hounds, whistling seals, and so on. A whistling seal sank a ship the other day.'[52]

What strikes the reader is the personality of the organizing intelligence behind the arrangement, and his musing, deliberate, and emphatically personal tone. He has supplied a kind of supervising narrator, simply through manipulation of tone and style. This could have an enduringly magnetic effect on the credulous (Kathleen Raine's lugubriously reverent introduction to a 1981 reprint is hard to read with a straight face). It also helps explain why a book which was nearly half reprints of already published material should have had the immense impact that it did; a phenomenon also created by its marvellous title. Rather like *The Invention of Tradition* in our own day, it put into currency a phrase which seemed to sum up what the era was waiting for.[53] For Yeats and his friends, 'Twilight' meant the hour before the dawn, with all the implication of an annunciation to come.

And the publication of the book, with the ripple-effect it created, proved a moment of annunciation in Yeats's own life. *The Celtic Twilight* was the book which brought Augusta Gregory to him; she met him first, briefly, a year after it was published, and their long friendship was forged when they met again in Galway in the summer of 1896. *The Celtic Twilight* had already inspired her to collect folklore around her home at Gort; collaboration with her would bring Yeats another stage of his journey, as he memorably recounts in the opening paragraphs of his beautiful essay on Swedenborg and mediums.

> Some fifteen years ago [actually 1897] I was in bad health and could not work, and Lady Gregory brought me from cottage to cottage while she began to collect stories, and presently when I was at work again she went on with her collection alone till it grew to be, so far as I know, the most considerable of its kind...As that ancient system of belief unfolded before us, with unforeseen probabilities and plausibilities, it was as though we had begun to live in a dream, and one day Lady Gregory said to me when we had passed an old man in the wood: 'That old man may know the secret of the ages.'[54]

Big Houses and hauntings recur, as in so many nineteenth-century novels. From there, Yeats's path projected forward into visionary experience, occultism, spiritism, psychic investigations, the arcane mental training courses of Theosophy, Rosicrucianism, the Order of the Golden Dawn, and all those activities which critics from Auden to Leavis found so distasteful. But *The Celtic Twilight* is also a book intimately concerned with Irish personality, national character, and peasant atmosphere. Crofton Croker and Lady Wilde had shaped his interpretation in several different ways. Moreover, the 1893 collection is simultaneously a record of the kind of inspiration that had come to him through his readings in Carleton, the Banims, Griffin, and so on—spurred by his anthologizing of fairytales, his investigations among those who held supernatural belief, and his taxonomies of fairy sociology. (This is all the more true of the second version in 1902.) And it bears witness to the themes which he was trying to build into his own occult novel, *The Speckled Bird*, during the 1890s—which, as with the equally troublesome unfinished dramatic poem *The Shadowy Waters*, tells us as much if not more about Yeats's creative processes than most of his achieved works. The way that 'hero tales' come to preoccupy him more than fairy legends similarly suggests an important development, reflected in the subjects he would choose for plays.[55]

This is also true of the remarkable occult short stories which he published in collected form as *The Secret Rose* in 1897: the visionary poetic power of Irish country people is here fused with a world of gods, heroes, ancient legends, and secret wisdoms. Devilish possession, Faustian bargains, sacred trees, symbolic animals, and fairy enchantments occur, as well as legendary demon lovers. The stories have a complex publishing history, and would be revised and rewritten many times throughout Yeats's life (notably in 1904, with Gregory's help); in the process they accumulated patterns and mythic levels of meaning as suggestive of Nietzsche and Wagner as of anything Irish.[56] Obsessive love for unearthly symbolic beauty is there from the beginning, reflecting the turmoil of Yeats's private life: he was by now firmly in thrall to Maud Gonne, which in turn affected his commitment to the politics of advanced nationalism. It is unknown if he ever went to the lengths of removing a strip of skin from a corpse in a graveyard at midnight and knotting it around her waist while she slept, but it may be doubted that he dared; not many men would.

The Secret Rose can be partly decoded in terms of his private obsessions. But in the first, simpler, appearance of the stories, they were closely connected with the long traditions of nineteenth-century Irish fiction, especially in its supernaturalist elements; stories such as 'The Wisdom of the King', for instance, derive directly from Lady Wilde's collections. It is also relevant that by the time he wrote these stories, the early 1890s, Yeats had not only been through tutorials with Madame Blavatsky and started passing examinations in the Order of the Golden Dawn; he had also been engaged in an intense bout of editorial work on William Blake's hitherto unknown visionary poem, *The Four Zoas* (with Edwin Ellis); and through this had been immersed in Swedenborg as well. The pages of a facsimile of Blake's *The Marriage of Heaven and Hell*, which Yeats used intensively, have survived, and are covered with his handwritten notes.[57] Along with esoteric reading in Rosicrucian and other texts, this is reflected in his short stories of the early 1890s, where alternative worlds are accessed as his heroic figures move through heavily symbolic landscapes. Swedenborg's *Heaven and Hell* lies behind much of Yeats's contemporary fiction, as it had lain behind Le Fanu's.

There are other links back to the inspirations of nineteenth-century Irish avatars in Yeats's early fiction. For instance, a central character in his stories, and one of Yeats's important alter egos, is the visionary and passionate wandering poet Red Hanrahan—directly derived from Yeats's readings about eighteenth-century Munster traditions. He had encountered this material in mid-nineteenth-century collections of Irish Jacobite songs and

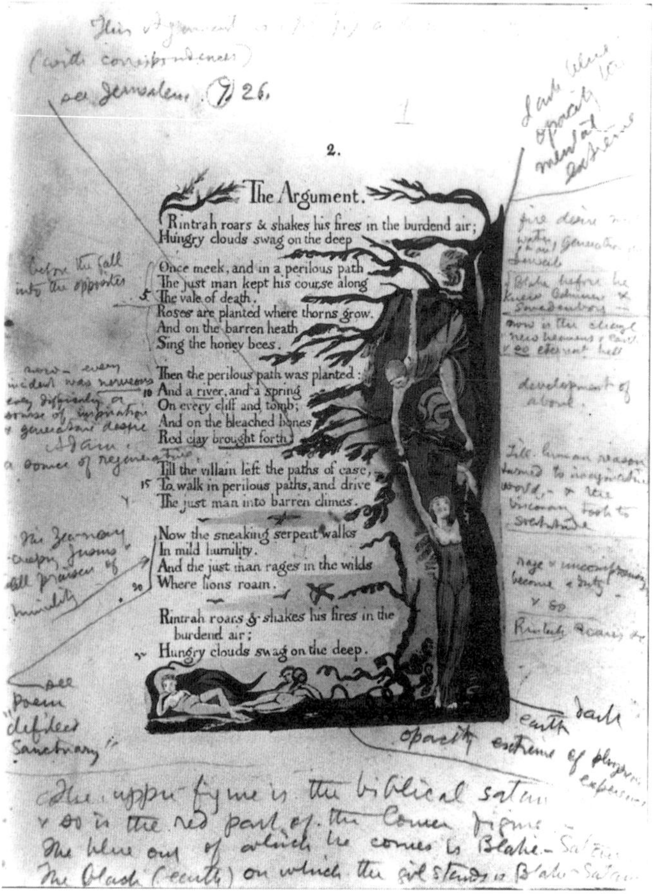

FIGURE 47 A page of William Blake's *Marriage of Heaven and Hell*, annotated by W. B. Yeats in the early 1890s

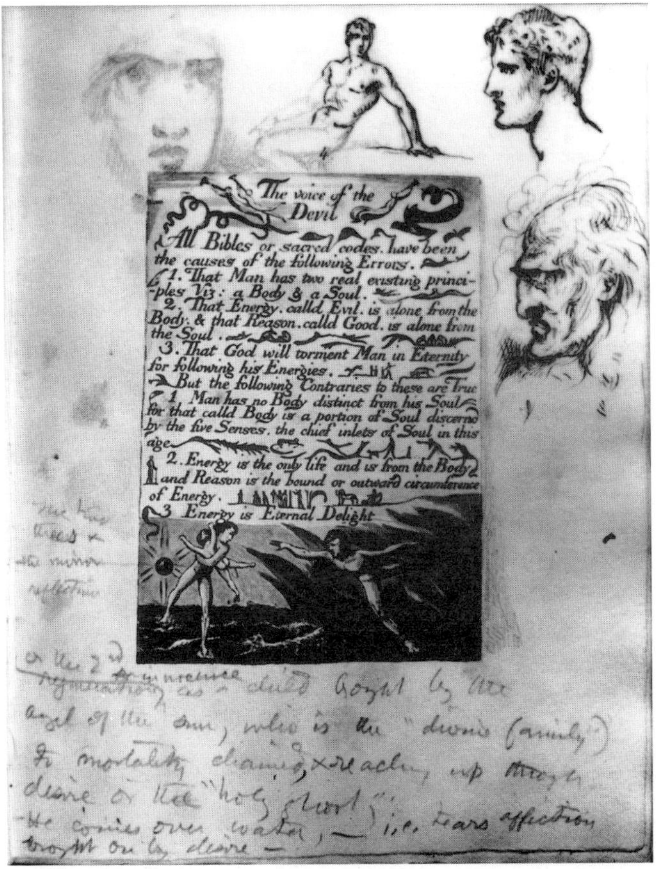

FIGURE 47 Continued

165

poets,[58] above all Mangan's *Poets and Poetry of Munster*—bringing us back once more to his influential crash course in the literature of the first Young Ireland movement. The stories also reflect material he accumulated for yet another anthology in the early 1890s, on 'Irish Adventurers' (outlaws, rogues, duellists, and so on), which was never completed. In the next phase of his career, Yeats's chosen invented alter ego would be the messianic magus Michael Robartes, rather than the country minstrel Red Hanrahan. By the end of the 1890s he had achieved magus status himself, and this is how the Irish artist Althea Gyles memorably drew him in 1898, in a proposed binding design for *The Wind Among the Reeds*, the consummate collection with which Yeats bade farewell to the nineties.[59] His later writings on Irish folklore (notably a series of six major articles between 1897 and 1902) owe

FIGURE 48 W. B. Yeats by Althea Gyles,
c. 1898

a great deal to collections published after 1890, and to Augusta Gregory's researches.

These reach beyond the period of his apprenticeship, and were written against a background of personal, intellectual, and spiritual upheaval. At the end of the 1890s Yeats's life underwent a series of crises which shaped his future fundamentally, and differently. But his own earlier explorations in folklore and Irish legend, like the inspirations that go back to *The Wanderings of Oisin*, and the reading in disputed Ossianic mythological sources that lies behind it, were not something he abandoned. This may stand as another Irish Victorian inheritance that marked his youth. *The Secret Rose*, he told O'Leary, was 'an honest attempt towards that aristocratic esoteric Irish literature, which has been my chief ambition'.[60] In a way, *The Wind Among the Reeds* in 1899 achieved this. But the preoccupation continued, and these keywords recur. 'There is no song or story handed down among the cottages', he wrote at the conclusion of the second edition of *The Celtic Twilight*,

> ...that has not words and thoughts to carry one as far, for though one can know but a little of their ascent, one knows that they ascend like medieval genealogies through unbroken dignities to the beginning of the world. Folk art is, indeed, the oldest of the aristocracies of thought, and because it refuses what is passing and trivial, the merely clever and pretty, as certainly as the vulgar and insincere, and because it has gathered into itself the simplest and the most unforgettable thoughts of the generations, it is the soil where all great art is rooted.[61]

This belief would stay with him and infuse many of the inspirational passions he would discover in later life—Indian traditional tales, Japanese ghost stories, and constant returns to the Cuchulain legends of early Irish tradition. The play *Purgatory*, mentioned in the last chapter, is one example; others include his very last poems.

It is worth pointing out that towards the end of his life, in the late 1930s, Yeats's work is generally seen as breaking out of genre in new and uncompromising ways—as indeed it does. But simultaneously it revisits and incorporates ballads, folktales, the vitality and earthiness of country superstitions and stories, and heroic legends—including those of the Fianna. Examples might include poems such as 'The Curse of Cromwell', 'The Supernatural Songs', 'The Pilgrim', 'Colonel Martin', 'John Kinsella's Lament for Mrs Mary Moore' 'The Black Tower', and 'Cuchulain Comforted'—these final two being the last poems he ever wrote. In all this work we can see him mining the riches of nineteenth-century Irish literary tradition which he had discovered in his apprenticeship from the 1880s. They also continued to inflect his idiosyncratic brand of cultural nationalism.

On 19 May 1893 Yeats gave a lecture called 'Nationality and Literature' in Dublin: an important statement of his beliefs about literature in Ireland and its relation to national identity.[62] It was also a salvo in his war with Duffy over the direction of the National Literary Society (who provided his audience). It is an important statement, not least because he is trying, not altogether successfully, to advance his theory of literature moving from the epic to the dramatic to the lyrical mood, situating Ireland in the epic stage and decadent England in the lyrical. This bears an odd relation to his own poetic achievement even by that date. But it is full of interest, not least in the metaphor he chooses for literary and cultural development: the growth into complex maturity of a great tree. '[Literature] in its youth is simple, and in its mid-period it grows in complexity, as does the tree when it puts forth many branches, and in its mature age it is covered by an innumerable variety of fruits and flowers and leaves of thought and experience...it must go through these periods no matter how greatly we long for finality, no matter how much we desire to make this or that stage permanent.'[63] This is an image which he would return to again and again, never more powerfully than thirty years later in 'Among School Children'.

> O chestnut tree, great rooted blossomer,
> Are you the leaf, the blossom, or the bole?[64]

For Yeats in 1893, Ireland *had* to be at the epic stage, as in Homeric Greece, because at that stage writers had 'for their

FIGURE 49 W. B. Yeats listening to Homer, as seen by Jack Yeats, *c.* 1887

material the national character, and the national history, and the national circumstances'. The epic and dramatic periods of a country's culture are necessarily national. Ireland in 1893 was

> a young nation with unexhausted material lying within us in our still unexpressed national character, about us in our scenery, and in the clearly marked outlines of our life, and behind us in our multitude of legends. Look at our literature and you will see that we are still in our epic or ballad period. All that is greatest in our literature is based upon legend—upon those tales which are made by no one man, but by the nation itself through a slow process of modification and adaption, to express its loves and its hates, its likes and its dislikes. Our best writers, De Vere, Ferguson, Allingham, Mangan, Davis, O'Grady, are all either ballad or epic writers, and all base their greatest work, if I except a song or two of Mangan's and Allingham's, upon legends and upon the fortunes of the nation. Alone, perhaps, among the nations of Europe we are in our ballad or epic age. The future will put some of our ballads with 'Percy's Reliques' and with the 'border' ballads, and at least one of our epic songs, the 'Conary' of Ferguson, among the simple, primitive poems of the world. Even the 'Spirit of the Nation' belongs to the epic age, for it deals with great National events.[65]

Responding to this speech, the Reverend J. F. Hogan remarked rather nervously that the speaker had undeniably made a mark upon Irish literature and was likely in future to make a deeper mark still. He was not wrong. But within a few years Yeats would change his mind about much of what he had said on that May evening in the Molesworth Hall, and many of his manifestos of the early twentieth century declare as much.

Even towards the end of that speech, an ambivalence creeps in, where he insists on the necessity to study from great international models, and decries local chauvinism and literary laziness; not only Blake but Flaubert are invoked as models. If Irish writers learn from the literatures of France and England to be supreme artists, then God will send them supreme inspiration—which is rather like trying to have it both ways.

But it is equally important to emphasize his belief that there existed to hand, in the literature of Victorian Ireland, an epic note—even in Davis's *Spirit of the Nation*. This is partly a political ploy, placing himself in direct line to the canonical inspiration of nationalist independence. At the same time it is a claim on Ferguson, O'Grady, and the spirit of Protestant Irishness. In his other writings of that energetic decade of his twenties, 1885 to 1895, he invoked—as we have seen—the supernaturalism of Lady Wilde and Le Fanu, the metrical daring of Mangan, the ironic realism of Edgeworth and Lawless, the 'fiery shorthand' of Carleton and Banim, and the complex and tangled root-systems of the nineteenth-century Irish literary tradition—which so many future critics would ignore when looking at Yeats's own remarkable trajectory. The dating and origins of the Literary Revival over which Yeats presided have been argued about back and forth, and Yeats's own importance and dominance debated; but not enough attention has been paid to the traditions out of which he came, as opposed to those which he invented for himself.

In April 1887, aged twenty-one, he had scrawled a mantra on the outside of a notebook (after several false attempts): 'Talent perceives difference, Genius Unity.'[66] This defined his own genius, and in hammering his thoughts into a unity he managed

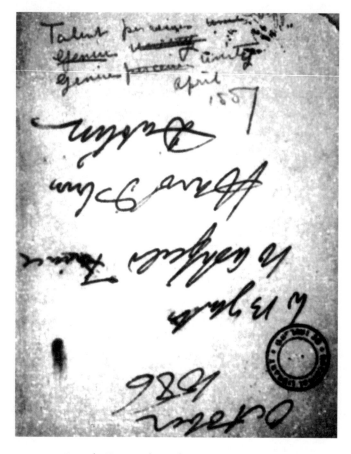

FIGURE 50   A note by Yeats on talent and genius, 1887

to despatch into obscurity a whole variety of predecessors and influences, some of whom have been resurrected from the smithy floor in the course of this book. This also implies the need to reconsider some themes and developments in the culture of nineteenth-century Ireland which have become lost to the retrospective view: the expectations of early Unionism, the interactions with contemporary Scottish literary history, the tangled course of Irish Romanticism, the deep roots of Irish supernaturalism, and the Irish taste for esoterica. The Literary Revival is, after all, part of Victorian Ireland—like the young Yeats himself. And, like Yeats, it looks back as well as forward.

NOTES

Introduction

1. E. H. Mikhail, *W. B. Yeats: Interviews and Recollections* (London, 1977, 2 vols.), Vol. II, p. 330.

2. 'The Poetry of W. B. Yeats', reprinted in J. Hall and Michael Steinman (eds.), *The Permanence of Yeats* (New York, 1950), p. 347. For Yeats and influence, see Richard Ellmann, *Eminent Domain: Yeats among Wilde, Joyce, Pound, Eliot and Auden* (Oxford, 1967), and Phillip L. Marcus, *Yeats and the Beginning of the Irish Renaissance* (Ithaca and London, 1970), particularly Chapter 1, 'Confrontations'.

3. To Ernest Boyd, 17 Aug. 1914, Healy Collection, Stanford University: quoted in my *W. B. Yeats: A Life. Vol. I: The Apprentice Mage 1865–1914* (Oxford, 1997), p. xxv.

4. For instance, W. J. McCormack's *Ascendancy and Tradition in Anglo-Irish Literary History from 1789 to 1939* (Oxford, 1985), and Malcolm Brown, *The Politics of Irish Literature from Thomas Davis to W. B. Yeats* (London, 1972). The exception is Joep Leerssen's endlessly stimulating *Remembrance and Imagination: Patterns in the Historical and Literary Representation of Ireland in the Nineteenth Century* (Cork, 1997), which brilliantly relates Yeats's early work on folklore and fairy faith to earlier traditions; but Leerssen, as he himself stresses, takes a highly

selective approach to the vast corpus of material at his disposal. I should nonetheless like to acknowledge his part in stimulating the lines of enquiry laid out in the present work.

5. Yeats's debts to his nineteenth-century predecessors might be read in similar terms to those stimulatingly established for Joyce by Emer Nolan in *Catholic Emancipations: Irish Fiction from Thomas Moore to James Joyce* (Syracuse, NY, 2007).

6. For varying reflections on this theme see for example my 'Protestant Magic: W. B. Yeats and the Spell of Irish History' in *Proceedings of the British Academy*, 75 (1989), pp. 243–66, reprinted in my *Paddy and Mr Punch: Connections in Irish and English History* (London, 1993), pp. 212–32; W. J. McCormack, *Sheridan Le Fanu and Victorian Ireland* (Oxford, 1980); Luke Gibbons, *Gaelic Gothic: Race, Colonization and Irish Culture* (Syracuse, 2006); Jarlath Killeen, *Gothic Ireland: Horror and the Irish Anglican Imagination in the Long Eighteenth Century* (Dublin, 2005).

7. F. R. Leavis, *English Literature in Our Time and the University* (London, 1969), pp. 136–7 (Yeats), p. 56 (Amis), p. 67 (Open University), p. 191 (American researchers).

8. Peter Allt and Russell K. Alspach (eds.), *The Variorum Edition of the Poems of W. B. Yeats* (third printing, New York, 1966), p. 66.

9. Louis MacNeice, *The Poetry of W. B. Yeats* (Oxford, 1941), p. 20.

10. George Bornstein and Hugh Witemayer (eds.), *Letters to the New Island: A New Edition* (London, 1989), p. xviii.

1 National Tales and National Futures in Ireland and Scotland after the Union

1. 'Novels of Irish life in the Nineteenth Century' (1897), reprinted in *Irish Books and Irish People* (London, 1919), pp. 7–22. For Gwynn see Colin Reid's pioneering doctoral thesis, 'The Political and Cultural

Life of Stephen Gwynn, with Particular Reference to the Period 1905–1926' (Queen's University, Belfast, 2008).

2. *Remembrance and Imagination*, p. 225; also see ibid., p. 35.

3. For allegory see especially Claire Connolly's introduction 'The Politics of Love in *The Wild Irish Girl*' in Sydney Owenson, *The Wild Irish Girl*, Claire Connolly and Stephen Copley (eds.) (London, 2000), p. xxx.

4. My thanks to Claire Connolly for this point.

5. See Tom Dunne (ed.), *The Writer as Witness: Literature as Historical Evidence*, Historical Studies XVI (Cork, 1987), notably the editor's essay 'The Best History of Nations: Lady Morgan's Novels', pp. 131–59, and Oliver MacDonagh's '*Sanditon*: A Regency Novel?', pp. 114–32. Another pioneering intervention was Tom Dunne's 'Haunted by History: Irish Romantic Writing 1800–1850' in R. Porter and M. Teich (eds.), *Romanticism in National Context* (Cambridge, 1988), pp. 68–91. It might be pointed out that even before Malcolm Brown's celebrated *The Politics of Irish Literature*, Thomas Flanagan's *The Irish Novelists* had opened up the subject in 1959. And after Brown, Barry Sloan's *The Pioneers of Anglo-Irish Fiction 1800–1850* (Totowa, NJ, 1987) made a valuable contribution, as did John Cronin's critical biography of Gerald Griffin (Cambridge, 1978), his editions of several of Griffin's novels, and his *The Anglo-Irish Novel. Vol. I: The Nineteenth Century* (Belfast, 1980).

6. See Kevin Whelan's preface to *The Wild Irish Girl*, Connolly and Copley (eds.). Less schematically, the new literary history is also determined to retrieve the peculiarities of Irish writing from a perspective tilted towards England, and to see Irish nineteenth-century fiction not as aspiring unsuccessfully to an English Great Tradition, but as addressing a different task and inhabiting a different zone.

7. Joe Cleary, 'The Nineteenth-Century Irish Novel: Notes and Speculations on Literary Historiography' in Jacqueline Belanger (ed.), *The Irish Novel in the Nineteenth Century: Facts and Fictions* (Dublin, 2005), pp. 203–4.

8. Katie Trumpener, *Bardic Nationalism: The Romantic Novel and the British Empire* (Princeton, 1997); Ina Ferris, *The Romantic National Tale and the Question of Ireland* (Cambridge, 2002); Claire Connolly's edition of *The Wild Irish Girl*, as above, her 'Irish Romanticism 1800–1829' in Margaret Kelleher and Philip O'Leary (eds.), *The Cambridge History of Irish Literature* (Cambridge, 2006), Vol. I, pp. 407–48, and her forthcoming Oxford volume on Irish Romantic fiction.

9. Benedict Anderson, *Imagined Communities: Reflections on the Origin and Spread of Nationalism* (London, 1983); for Anderson's own hybrid Irishness see his appealing memoir 'Selective Kinship' in *Dublin Review*, 10 (Spring 2003), pp. 5–29. Also see Timothy Brennan, 'The National Longing for Form' in Homi K. Bhabha (ed.), *Nation and Narration* (London, 1990), pp. 44–70.

10. Terry Eagleton, *Heathcliff and the Great Hunger: Studies in Irish Culture* (London, 1995), p. 9.

11. See Dunne, 'Haunted by History' in Porter and Teich (eds.), *Romanticism in National Context*, and Ian Duncan, 'Ireland, Scotland and the Materials of Romanticism' in David Duff and Catherine Jones (eds.), *Scotland, Ireland and the Romantic Aesthetic* (Lewisburg, Pa., 2007), pp. 258–78; and Emer Nolan, *Catholic Emancipations: Irish Fiction from Thomas Moore to James Joyce* (Syracuse, NY, 2007), especially pp. 43–52.

12. Pioneered by Rolf Loeber and Magda Stouthamer-Loeber, made accessible by the invaluable Field Day anthologies of Irish writing, and now magisterially presented in Rolf Loeber and Magda Stouthamer-Loeber with Anne M. Burnham, *A Guide to Irish Fiction 1650–1900* (Dublin, 2006). The *Castle Rackrent* origin-legend was first queried by W. J. McCormack in *Ascendancy and Tradition in Anglo-Irish Literary History from 1789 to 1939* (Oxford, 1985), Chapter 3.

13. See for instance Robert Crawford, *Scotland's Books* (London, 2007), and Murray Pittock, *Scottish and Irish Romanticism* (Oxford, 2008).

14. See especially Clare O'Halloran, 'Irish Re-creations of the Gaelic Past: The Challenge of Macpherson's *Ossian*', *Past and Present*, 124

(1989), pp. 69–85, and *Golden Ages and Barbarous Nations: Antiquarian Debate and Cultural Politics in Ireland c. 1750–1800* (Cork, 2004).

15. For varying reactions and interpretations see *inter alia* Fiona Stafford, *The Sublime Savage: A Study of James Macpherson and the Poems of Ossian* (Edinburgh, 1989); Daffyd R. Moore, 'The Critical Response to Ossian's Romantic Bequest' in Gerard Carruthers and Alan Rawes (eds.), *English Romanticism and the Celtic World* (Cambridge, 2003); Colin Kidd, *British Identities before Nationalism: Ethnicity and Nationhood in the Atlantic World 1600–1900* (Cambridge, 1999) and *Subverting Scotland's Past: Whig Historians and the Creation of an Anglo-British Identity 1698–1830* (Cambridge, 1993); Hugh Trevor-Roper, *The Invention of Scotland: Myth and History* (London, 2008).

16. Quoted in Neil McCaw (ed.), *Writing Irishness in Nineteenth-Century British Culture* (Aldershot, 2004), p. 19.

17. W. E. H. Lecky, *History of Ireland in the Eighteenth Century* (5 vols., London, 1892), Vol. I, p. 1.

18. *Quarterly Review*, 4 (1810), quoted in Duff and Jones (eds.), *Scotland, Ireland and the Romantic Aesthetic*, p. 20.

19. Peter Garside, 'Popular Fiction and National Tale: Hidden Origins of Scott's *Waverley*', *Nineteenth-Century Literature*, 46, 1 (June 1991), esp. pp. 49–53; also see his edition of *Waverley* for Edinburgh University Press (2007).

20. Seamus Deane, *Strange Country: Modernity and Nationhood in Irish Writing since 1790* (Oxford, 1997), pp. 32–3. Ian Duncan makes a similar point about Irish/Scottish futures from another angle in 'Ireland, Scotland and the Materials of Romanticism' in Duff and Jones (eds.), *Scotland, Ireland and the Romantic Aesthetic*; also see his *Scott's Shadow: The Novel in Romantic Edinburgh* (Princeton, 2007).

21. See Cliona Ó Gallchoir, *Maria Edgeworth: Women, Enlightenment and Nation* (Dublin, 2007), for an extended and suggestive treatment of this novel.

22. *Castle Rackrent* [Oxford English Novels series] (Oxford, 1969), p. 5.

23. *Redgauntlet* has been 'mapped' against James Hogg's *Private Memoirs and Confessions of a Justified Sinner* by Ian Duncan in *Scott's Shadow* and Fiona Robertson in *Legitimate Histories: Scott, Gothic and the Authorities of Fiction* (Oxford, 1994), but the Edgeworth text seems far closer.

24. Scott to John Richardson, 16 Sept. 1825, J. G. Grierson *et al.*, *Letters of Sir Walter Scott* (12 vols., London, 1832–8), pp. ix, 232.

25. D. J. O'Donoghue, *Sir Walter Scott's Tour in Ireland in 1825* (Dublin, 1905), p. 25.

26. See Seamus Deane, 'Irish National Character 1790–1900' in Dunne, *The Writer as Witness*, pp. 90–113; also, for non-British reactions in the 1830s, Alexis de Tocqueville, *Journeys to England and Ireland*, J. P. Mayer (ed.) (London, 1958), pp. 118–92, where Irish mores are repeatedly compared to French rather than English ones; and Gustave de Beaumont, *Ireland: Social, Political and Religious*, W. C. Taylor (ed.), with an introduction by Tom Garvin and Andreas Hess (Cambridge, Mass., 2006).

27. O'Donoghue, *Sir Walter Scott's Tour in Ireland in 1825*, pp. 73–5.

28. Clare O'Halloran, 'Harping on the Past: Translating Antiquarian Learning into Popular Culture in Early Nineteenth-Century Ireland' in Melissa Calaresu, Filippo de Vivo, and Joan Pau Rubies (eds.), *Exploring Cultural History: Essays in Honour of Peter Burke* (Farnham, Surrey, 2010), pp. 327–43 (my thanks to Dr O'Halloran for this reference); and Garside, 'Popular Fiction and National Tale', p. 51.

29. Quoted in Duff and Jones (eds.), *Scotland, Ireland and the Romantic Aesthetic*, pp. 20–1.

30. Pittock, *Scottish and Irish Romanticism*, pp. 189–90, 203ff.; James Anderson, *Sir Walter Scott and History* (Edinburgh, 1981), p. 105; Julia Meldon D'Arcy, *Subversive Scott: The Waverley Novels and Scottish Nationalism* (Reykjavik, 2005).

31. The case is not strengthened by the same authority's admission that Scott's use of Enlightenment historiography was weakened by his

unfamiliarity with national questions outside Britain: Pittock, *Scottish and Irish Romanticism*, p. 210.

32. Ó Gallchoir, *Maria Edgeworth, passim*.

33. Deane, *Strange Country*, pp. 30–1 and 135; Kevin Whelan's preface to *The Wild Irish Girl*, Connolly and Copley (eds.), pp. xiii–xv, xxi–xxii.

34. Seamus Deane, *Strange Country*, pp. 37–8.

35. *Journeys to England and Ireland*, pp. 157–8. De Tocqueville instanced as reasons behind the Irish case religious difference coinciding with class difference, the vividness of the memory of conquest, and the deliberate maintenance of poverty. See also J. S. Mill's thoughtful analysis of Irish 'difference' in his writings of the 1860s.

36. Seamus Deane, *Strange Country*, p. 39.

37. See Timothy Webb, ' "A Great Theatre of Outrage and Disorder": Figuring Ireland in the *Edinburgh Review* 1802–1829' in Duncan Wu and Massimiliano Demata (eds.), *British Romanticism and the Edinburgh Review: Bicentenary Essays* (London, 2003), pp. 58ff.

38. *Edinburgh Review*, 43 (Feb. 1826), pp. 356–72: discussed in Ronan Kelly, *Bard of Erin: The Life of Thomas Moore* (Dublin, 2008), p. 434.

39. Nolan, *Catholic Emancipations*, Chapters 1–2.

40. See Marilyn Butler, 'Irish Culture and Scottish Enlightenment: Maria Edgeworth's Histories of the Future' in Stefan Collini, Richard Whatmore, and Brian Young (eds.), *Economy, Polity and Society: British Intellectual History 1750–1950* (Cambridge, 2000), pp. 158–80.

41. See Webb, ' "A Great Theatre of Outrage and Disorder" ', pp. 70–1.

42. *Edinburgh Review*, 34, 68 (Nov. 1820), p. 334.

43. Webb, ' "A Great Theatre of Outrage and Disorder" ', pp. 74–5.

44. *Edinburgh Review*, 34, 68 (Nov. 1820), p. 334.

45. 'Gallery of Illustrious Irishmen. III: Berkeley' in *Dublin University Magazine*, 7 (Apr. 1836), pp. 437–8; quoted in Joseph Spence, 'The Philosophy of Irish Toryism 1833–1852: A Study of Reactions to Liberal Reformism in Ireland in the Generation between the First

Reform Act and the Famine, with Especial Reference to Expressions of National Feeling among the Protestant Ascendancy' (Ph.D., University of London, 1991), p. 185.

46. Joep Leerssen and Manfred Beller (eds.), *Imagology: The Cultural Construction and Literary Representation of National Character – A Critical Survey* (Amsterdam, 2007), p. 19.

47. Quoted in Pittock, *Scottish and Irish Romanticism*, p. 187.

48. Ian Duncan suggests this in Duff and Jones (eds.), *Scotland, Ireland and the Romantic Aesthetic*, pp. 258ff.; see also pp. 265–6.

49. Kidd, *British Identities*, pp. 139–40, 160–1.

50. Eagleton, *Heathcliff and the Great Hunger*, p. 15.

51. Emer Nolan's *Catholic Emancipations* is a notable exception.

52. See Graham McMaster, *Scott and Society* (Cambridge, 1981), introduction and pp. 12ff., 26ff., 106. In *Redgauntlet* one might instance the Quaker 'improver' of his lands, the opposing alternative moral economy of the archaic net-fishers, the civil but colourless contrast of England across the Solway. Here again the parallels with Edgeworth's *Ormond* are sharply distinct.

53. *The Boyne Water* has been usefully reprinted with an introduction and glossary by Bernard Escarbelt (CERIUL Anglo-Irish Texts, Patrick Rafroidi (ed.), Lille, 1976) and is discussed at length in James M. Cahalan, *Great Hatred, Little Room: The Irish Historical Novel* (Dublin, 1983), Chapter 3, and by Emer Nolan in 'Banim and the Historical Novel' in Belanger (ed.), *The Irish Novel in the Nineteenth Century*, pp. 80–93, and *Catholic Emancipations*, Chapter 2.

54. Trumpener, *Bardic Nationalism*, pp. 101, 130–2, 141ff., 156.

55. See *Catholic Emancipations*, pp. 11ff., especially p. 26.

56. Roger O'Connor's critique, quoted in Nolan, *Catholic Emancipations*, p. 13.

57. There is an excellent discussion of the text in Kelly, *Bard of Erin*, pp. 395–403, and an important recent Field Day edition by Seamus

Deane and Emer Nolan (Dublin, 2009). (Kelly convincingly argues that Moore's inflammatory youthful rhetoric, in productions like 'Imitation of Ossian', was cut short by 1798.)

58. Pittock, *Scottish and Irish Romanticism*, p. 112.

59. *Florence MacCarthy*, quoted in Trumpener, *Bardic Nationalism*, p. 142.

60. See particularly the work of Linda Colley: *Britons: Forging the Nation 1707–1837* (London, 1992), *Captives: British Empire and the World 1600–1850* (London, 2002), *The Ordeal of Elizabeth Marsh* (London, 2007).

61. Ferris, *The Romantic National Tale and the Question of Ireland*, p. 17.

62. For a venerable but still acute survey see R. D. Collison Black, *Economic Thought and the Irish Question 1817–1870* (Cambridge, 1960). Pioneering surveys include Wakefield's *Account of Ireland, Statistical and Political* (1812) and Thomas Newenham, *Statistical and Historical Inquiry into the Population of Ireland* (1808). Also see Peter Gray, *Famine, Land and Politics: British Government and Irish Society 1843–1850* (Dublin, 1999).

63. Ferris, *The Romantic National Tale and the Question of Ireland*, p. 45, paraphrasing Trumpener.

64. See John MacQueen, *The Rise of the Historical Novel: The Enlightenment and Scottish Literature* (Edinburgh, 1989), and Cahalan, *Great Hatred, Little Room*.

65. Pittock, *Scottish and Irish Romanticism*, p. 74.

66. Trumpener, *Bardic Nationalism*, pp. 145–6. For *The Nowlans* see Nolan, *Catholic Emancipations*, pp. 59ff.

67. These authors also present problems for Joe Cleary's otherwise subtle and well-founded critique of nineteenth-century Irish literary history and historiography, wherein he defines Irish literature in English as conforming to the mode of 'other settler colonies...a dependent offshoot of the literature of a European mother country...developed...primarily by intellectuals descended from what was historically a "creole" colonial settler community'. Moore,

Carleton, and Banim are co-opted into this descent: 'writers from the various classes of the "native" community in the colonies, distanced by education and acculturation from the masses of their "own" community...invariably took Europe or the imperial "mother-country" as the lodestar of cultural reference' (Cleary, 'The Nineteenth-Century Irish Novel: Some Notes and Speculations' in Belanger (ed.), *The Irish Novel in the Nineteenth Century*, p. 211). While this is suggestive, it is rather at odds with the actual social background and perceived self-image of these writers.

68. For reflections of this vitality see Claire Connolly, ' "I Accuse Miss Owenson": *The Wild Irish Girl* as Media Event', *Colby Quarterly*, 36, 2 (June 2000), pp. 98–115, and 'Theater and Nation in Irish Romanticism: The Tragic Dramas of Charles Robert Maturin and Richard Lalor Sheil', *Éire-Ireland*, 41, 3–4 (Fall/Winter 2006), pp. 185–214; Christopher Morash, *A History of the Irish Theatre 1601–2000* (Cambridge, 2000); J. R. R. Adams, *The Printed Word and the Common Man: Popular Culture in Ulster 1700–1900* (Belfast, 1997); Niall Ó Ciosáin, *Print and Popular Culture in Ireland 1750–1850* (London, 1997).

69. See Pittock, *Scottish and Irish Romanticism*, p. 90, and McMaster, *Scott and Society*, p. 57.

70. While Trumpener's *Bardic Nationalism* is in many ways a *tour de force*, her statement 'down to the present day English detachment and disdain towards Ireland conceals a will to dominate, motivated both by envy at the cultural vitality of the conquered and by a deep fear of England's own innate inferiority' (p. 7) seems rather over-egging the pudding.

71. See Terry Eagleton's afterword in Belanger (ed.), *The Irish Novel in the Nineteenth Century*, p. 228.

72. W. B. Yeats to Father Matthew Russell, early Dec. 1889, John Kelly (ed.) with Eric Domvile, *The Collected Letters of W. B. Yeats. Vol. I: 1865–1895* (Oxford, 1986), pp. 198–200.

73. 'First Principles' in *Samhain* (1908), reprinted in W. B. Yeats, *Explorations* (London, 1962), p. 235.

74. '...invented by political journalists and forensic historians'. This comes from his article 'Irish National Literature II: Contemporary Prose Writers' (1895), reprinted in John P. Frayne (ed.), *Uncollected Prose by W. B. Yeats. Vol. I: First Reviews and Articles 1886–1896* (London, 1970), p. 370.

2 The First Romantics: Young Irelands between Catholic Emancipation and the Famine

1. Kenneth J Fielding and David R. Sorensen (eds.), *Jane Carlyle: Newly Selected Letters* (Aldershot, 2004), p. 118. Also Charles Gavan Duffy, *Conversations with Carlyle* (London, 1892), pp. 8–10. They first met in Apr. On 12 May Carlyle had written a long letter to Duffy about the *Nation*, and 'Justice for Ireland'. John O'Hagan to C. G. Duffy, 17 Jan. 1845 [but clearly 1846], NLI MS 5756, reports affectionate enquiries from Carlyle via Frederick Lucas, who first introduced them – as well as high praise from Carlyle for Mitchel's review of his *Cromwell*. Carlyle subsequently enlisted Duffy to help with the Irish sections of the second edition. For Carlyle and Young Ireland, see Owen Dudley Edwards, ' "True Thomas": Carlyle, Young Ireland and the Legacy of Millennialism' in David Sorensen and Rodger L. Tarr (eds.), *The Carlyles at Home and Abroad* (Aldershot, 2006), pp. 61–76.

2. Alan Shelston (ed.), *Thomas Carlyle: Selected Writings* (Harmondsworth, 1971), pp. 169–70. It should be remembered that this alarming spectre is clearly caused by bad government and endemic poverty: the section 'Finest Peasantry in the World' is violently Saxonist but also oddly compassionate and overwhelmingly anti-Utilitarian. Laisser-faire principles are the target, not Irish inferiority.

3. The traditional view of Carlyle's anti-Irish tirades as evidence of simple racism may be found in L. P. Curtis, *Apes and Angels: The Irishman in Victorian Caricature* (revised edition, Washington, DC, 1997), p. 114, and Cora Kaplan, 'White, Black and Green: Racializing Irishness in Victorian England' in Peter Gray (ed.), *Victoria's Ireland? Irishness and Britishness 1837–1900* (Dublin, 2004). It has been powerfully contested by John Morrow, 'Thomas Carlyle, "Young Ireland" and the "Condition of Ireland Question"', *Historical Journal*, 51, 3 (2008), pp. 643–67. Also see Julie M. Dugger, 'Black Ireland's Race: Thomas Carlyle and the Young Ireland Movement', *Victorian Studies*, 48, 3 (Spring 2006), pp. 461–85.

4. *Conversations with Carlyle*, p. 6.

5. J. A. Froude's 1883 edition of *Letters and Memorials of Jane Welsh Carlyle*, quoted in *Conversations with Carlyle*, p. 1.

6. 19 Jan. 1846, in Charles Richard Sanders, K. J. Fielding, Ian Campbell, *et al.* (eds.), *Collected Letters of Thomas and Jane Welsh Carlyle* (Edinburgh and Durham, NC, 1970–), Vol. XX (1993), p. 106.

7. David A. Wilson, *Thomas D'Arcy Magee. Vol. I: Passion, Reason and Politics 1825–1857* (Kingston, Ontario, 2008), pp. 110–11, for a good commentary. Also Helen Mulvey, *Thomas Davis and Ireland: A Biographical Study* (Washington, DC, 2003), Chapter 6.

8. Not at all, for instance, in Seamus Deane's *Strange Country*.

9. See Matthew Kelly, *The Fenian Ideal and Irish Nationalism 1882–1916* (Woodbridge, 2006), Chapter 1, for the Young Ireland societies of the 1880s.

10. For Tennent see John Bew, *The Glory of Being Britons: Civic Unionism in Nineteenth-Century Belfast* (Dublin, 2008), and for Croker, Robert Portsmouth, *John Wilson Croker: Irish Ideas and the Invention of Modern Conservatism 1800–1835* (Dublin, 2010), and his unpublished article 'A Neglected Tradition of Irish Political Thought: John Wilson Croker, the Irish "Spin Doctors", and the Invention of the

Conservative Party 1805–1835': my thanks to Dr Portsmouth for showing me this. His work establishes that Croker, in fact, usually presented as a splenetic reactionary, can be seen as an active pro-Emancipationist, and a voice preaching reconciliation in national interests during the early years of the Union.

11. Spence, 'The Philosophy of Irish Toryism 1833–1852', pp. 41ff.; the article appeared in Vol. VI (1835).

12. 'The Whig Government of Ireland', *DUM*, 1 (Apr.1833), p. 459.

13. See Terry Eagleton, *Scholars and Rebels in Nineteenth-Century Ireland* (Oxford, 2000), pp. 130–1, and Stiofán Ó Cadhla, *Civilizing Ireland: Ordnance Survey 1824–1842 – Ethnography, Cartography, Translation* (Dublin, 2007); cf. Eve Patten, *Samuel Ferguson and the Culture of Nineteenth-Century Ireland* (Dublin, 2006), pp. 8off., for a discussion of this critique, and J. H. Andrews's classic and indispensable study, *A Paper Landscape: The Ordnance Survey in Nineteenth-Century Ireland* (Oxford, 1975).

14. John N. Molony, *A Soul Came into Ireland: Thomas Davis 1814–1845 – A Biography* (Dublin, 1996), p. 144. More analytically, David Dwan's valuable recent study of Young Ireland stresses the input of classically derived civic and humanist principles as part of the Young Ireland cultural enterprise: David Dwan, *The Great Community: Culture and Nationalism in Ireland* (Dublin, 2008), p. 3.

15. Published the same year as Carlyle's *Chartism*, this took a very different line, laying Ireland's problems at the door of English rule and the landlord system, and was a sensational success in France; for an illuminating recent edition see Gustave de Beaumont, *Ireland, Social, Political, and Religious*, W. C. Taylor (ed. and trans.), with an introduction by Tom Garvin and Andreas Hess (London and Cambridge, Mass., 2006). For Young Ireland's cult of de Tocqueville see Dwan, *The Great Community*, pp. 145–6, and Charles Gavan Duffy, *Four Years of Irish History 1845–1849* (London, 1883), Vol. I, p. 57.

16. *Nation*, 5 Apr. 1845.

17. Gerald Griffin's impressive contemporary novel, *The Collegians*, ends
    with the 1828 elections; his subsequent historical novel, *The Invasion*,
    exhausted him and he retired to a religious institution. As discussed
    in the last chapter, John Banim's *The Boyne Water* is similarly writ-
    ten against the background of the Catholic Emancipation struggle:
    this clearly informs its seventeenth-century plot, which interestingly
    avoids the usual symmetrical happy-marriage resolution.

18. *Nation*, 19 Aug. 1843.

19. Jeanne Sheehy, *The Rediscovery of Ireland's Past: The Celtic Revival
    1800–1830* (London, 1980), for many examples.

20. *Nation*, 21 Oct. 1843.

21. F. Schlegel in *Athenäum* (1798), quoted in Roy Porter and Mikulas
    Teich (eds.), *Romanticism in National Context* (Cambridge, 1980),
    p. 114.

22. He put this most pungently in his review of Hardiman's *Irish
    Minstrelsy*:

    > We will leave the idiotic brawler, the bankrupt and fraudulent dema-
    > gogue, the crawling incendiary, the scheming, Jesuitical, ambitious
    > priest – that perverse rabble in [on]whom the mire in which they have
    > wallowed for the last quarter of a century, has caked into a crust like
    > the armour of the Egyptian beast, till they are case-hardened invulner-
    > ably in the filth of habitual impudence, ingratitude, hypocrisy, envy and
    > malice; so that it were but a vain defilement of aught manly or honour-
    > able to advance against such panoply of every foul component – we
    > will leave them to their employment of reproach and agitation, and
    > sing the song of men who might well rise from honourable graves, and
    > affright the midnight echoes of Aughrim or Benburb with their lamen-
    > tations, if they could know that their descendants were fools enough to
    > be led by such a directory of knaves and cowards.

    Quoted in Malcolm Brown, *Samuel Ferguson* (Lewisburg, Pa., 1973),
    p. 49.

23. See 'The Story of Ireland' in my *The Irish Story: Telling Tales and Making It Up in Ireland* (London, 2001), pp. 1–22.

24. Review of Hardiman, quoted in Brown, *Samuel Ferguson*, p. 47.

25. [Thomas Wallis (ed.)], *The Poems of Thomas Davis: Now First Collected, with Notes and Historical Illustrations* (Dublin, 1846), p. 28.

26. Spence, 'The Philosophy of Irish Toryism 1833–1852', Chapter 6, for a brilliant treatment of this genre, which includes William Maxwell's *O'Hara* (1825), a novel about the 1798 Rising, which argued strongly for Catholic Emancipation; Sheridan Le Fanu's early stories; and Mortimer O'Sullivan's *The Nevilles of Garretstown* (1844).

27. Charles Gavan Duffy, *Young Ireland: A Fragment of Irish History 1840–1850* (London, 1880), pp. 501–2. See Spence, 'The Philosophy of Irish Toryism 1833–1852', p. 361, for the *DUM* writers and Ulster.

28. Spence, 'The Philosophy of Irish Toryism 1833–1852', pp. 300ff., compares the Banim and Butt works.

29. For the Butt text see *DUM*, 9, 31 (Mar. 1837), pp. 365–76, reprinted in Seamus Deane, Andrew Carpenter, and Jonathan Williams (eds.), *The Field Day Anthology of Irish Writing* (3 vols., Derry, 1991), Vol. I, pp. 1,200–12. Spence convincingly attributes this to Butt rather than to Mortimer O'Sullivan, as claimed by the *Wellesley Index*. For one of those echoes from the other side, see the O'Connellite Thomas O'Hagan's 1831 address to the Belfast Historical Society: 'A peculiar literature is the noblest possession that can belong to a people. It is the outbreathing of the soul, the manifestation of their intellectual power.' Counting for far more than territorial aggrandizement or the accumulation of wealth, O'Hagan held that a national literature should 'take its form and impress from the spirit of the people – a literature which is stamped, in clear and lustrous characters, by the genius of our country as her own' (quoted in Patten, *Samuel Ferguson and the Culture of Nineteenth-Century Ireland*, p. 38).

30. Spence, 'The Philosophy of Irish Toryism 1833–1852', pp. 182ff. The *Dublin Penny Journal* had anticipated this with a series of 'National Biographies' in 1832–3 and the *Nation* would copy it.

31. See Tom Dunne, 'Chivalry, the Harp and Maclise's Contribution to the Creation of National Identity' in Peter Murray (ed.), *Daniel Maclise 1806–1870: Romancing the Past* (Kinsale, 2008), pp. 38–51.

32. Ibid., pp. 39, 50, and 74 (on *The Marriage of Strongbow and Aoife*).

33. As shown by Bernard O'Donoghue, 'Poetry in Ireland' in Joe Cleary and Claire Connolly (eds.), *The Cambridge Companion to Modern Irish Culture* (Cambridge, 2005), pp. 173–89, and Matthew Campbell, 'Poetry in English 1830–1890: From Catholic Emancipation to the Fall of Parnell' in Kelleher and O'Leary (eds.), *The Cambridge History of Irish Literature*, Vol. I, especially pp. 504–15.

34. See Dunne, 'Haunted by History' in Porter and Teich (eds.), *Romanticism in National Context*, pp. 68–91, which includes an important reassessment of Moore. Moore's satiric verse has also been revalued: see Jane Moore, 'Thomas Moore as Irish Satirist' in Duff and Jones (eds.), *Scotland, Ireland and the Romantic Aesthetic*, pp. 152–71.

35. See Harry White, *Music and the Irish Literary Imagination* (Oxford, 2008), Chapter 1.

36. 29 Oct. 1842; also see 24 Dec. 1842. Reprinted in Deane, Carpenter, and Williams (eds.), *The Field Day Anthology*, Vol. I, pp. 1,250–4.

37. See their 'Literary Absentees: Irish Women Writers in Nineteenth-Century England' in Belanger (ed.), *The Irish Novel in the Nineteenth Century*, pp. 169ff.

38. See Duffy, *Young Ireland*, pp. 670–1, for caustic remarks on the other Duffy.

39. Though for penetrating remarks about Mangan's self-parody see Melissa Fegan, *Literature and the Irish Famine 1845–1919* (Oxford,

2002), Chapter 6; also Deane, *Strange Country*, pp. 122–6, on Mangan's reputation.

40. Besides *Young Ireland*, see also *Four Years of Irish History 1845–1849* (London, 1883) and *My Life in Two Hemispheres* (2 vols., London, 1903). Duffy's correspondence in the National Library of Ireland equally reflects a chatty and irreverent café culture (especially Mac-Nevin's letters in MS 5756).

41. Patten, *Samuel Ferguson and the Culture of Nineteenth-Century Ireland*, p. 30.

42. Ibid., p. 100.

43. See *Nation*, 4 Mar. 1843.

44. Dwan, *The Great Community*, pp. 58–9, for useful quotes showing the latter tendency.

45. [Thomas Wallis (ed.)], *The Poems of Thomas Davis*, p. xiii. Scott's remarks in his introduction to the first edition of *The Bridal of Triermain* (1813) are apposite here.

> Poets, under various denominations of Bards, Scalds, Chroniclers, and so forth, are the first historians of all nations. Their intention is to relate the events they have witnessed, or the traditions that have reached them; and they clothe the relation in rhyme, merely as the means of rendering it more solemn in the narrative or more easily committed to memory. But, as the poetical historian improves in the art of conveying information, the authenticity of his narrative unavoidably declines. He is tempted to dilate and dwell upon the events that are interesting to his imagination, and, conscious how indifferent his audience is to the naked truth of his poem, his history gradually becomes a romance.

Quoted in Andrew Nicholson, 'Byron and the "Ariosto of the North"' in Carruthers and Rawes (eds.), *English Romanticism and the Celtic World*, p. 138.

46. It seems that Davis may have sometimes pursued these questions in his non-poetic persona as well, at least to judge from his

correspondence with William Tait, a radical newspaper proprietor in Britain, who advised peaceful agitation instead. See Molony, *A Soul Came into Ireland*, p. 181.

47. Duffy, *Young Ireland*, p. 563 (quoting MacNevin). See 'Pastimes' chapter in ibid. for useful observations.

48. 'A Song for the Irish Militia', [Thomas Wallis (ed.)], *The Poems of Thomas Davis*, p. 21.

49. Nor was the implication of Davis's speech in Apr. 1845 launching the '82 Club', where he related artistic achievement to national freedom and asked how anyone who had 'never looked on the "sight entrancing" of citizens arrayed in arms for freedom' could 'reach the rank of a national artist'. Cf. editorial in the *Nation* of 29 Apr. 1843 on 'Our Nationality'. 'Twenty thousand Tipperary men, who would as soon, if called on, pay their blood as their subscriptions, would not form a bad National Guard for Ireland.' See also Dwan, *The Great Community*, pp. 70–1, on this inconsistency – which might also reflect a muted disagreement between Duffy and Davis.

50. D. O. Maddyn, *Ireland and Its Rulers* (3 vols., London, 1843–4), Vol. III, p. 245, quoted in Mulvey, *Thomas Davis and Ireland*, p. 227.

51. These began in the issue of 17 Dec. 1842.

52. See editorials of 25 Feb. and 8 Apr. 1843.

53. Fegan, *Literature and the Irish Famine*; Christopher Morash, *The Hungry Voice: The Poetry of the Irish Famine* (Dublin, 1989) and *Writing the Irish Famine* (Oxford, 1985).

54. 6 Feb. 1847; see Dwan, *The Great Community*, p. 62.

55. 1849; discussed in Patten, *Samuel Ferguson and the Culture of Nineteenth-Century Ireland*, pp. 118–19. Butt's last lecture declared that 'it is impossible in any inquiry of political economy, to escape from the grand problem of the social system... what is the right, and what is the [actual] position of the poor?' These lectures were gathered in *Protection to Home Industry: Some Cases of Its Advantage Considered*

(Dublin, 1846), discussed in Spence, 'The Philosophy of Irish Tory-ism 1833–1852', pp. 239–48.

56. See Patten, *Samuel Ferguson and the Culture of Nineteenth-Century Ireland*, pp. 108–9; also Lady Ferguson, *Sir Samuel Ferguson in the Ireland of His Day* (2 vols., London, 1896), Vol. I, pp. 123–6.

57. 13 May 1848.

58. Mitchel's memorable phrase: see *Nation*, 27 May 1848.

59. *Nation*, 4 Mar. 1848, 18 Sept. 1847; see Dwan, *The Great Community*, p. 145.

60. 'Meagher's Memory of Forty-Eight', *Waterford Chronicle*, 15 Feb. 1851, quoted in John M. Hearne and Rory T. Cornish (eds.), *Thomas Francis Meagher: The Making of an Irish-American* (Dublin, 2006), p. 58. The *Nation*, 22 July 1848, confirms his outfit: 'a green frock [-coat], lined with white silk, a rich tricolour sash with rosette and heavy gold fringe, a handsome military cap and white trousers'.

61. Carlyle to O'Hagan, 2 Apr. 1849, *Collected Letters*, Vol. XXIV (1995), pp. 1–2.

62. *Nation*, 10 June 1848.

63. Carlyle to Duffy, 6 Feb. 1853, *Collected Letters*, Vol XXVIII (2000), pp. 33–4 ('. . . a thing which any carpenter with sixpence worth of nails can knock together for you in an hour or two; which might hold 150 or 200 volumes – and which would be a small but real comfort to me to know doing service for some friendly Christian in this manner!').

64. Clarendon's fury is recorded in a letter to the prime minister, Russell, in ibid., Vol. XXIV (1995), p. 101, fn. 2.

65. An instructive comparison from another British observer might be Anthony Trollope's early Irish novels, also written in the 1840s; *The Kellys and the O'Kellys* opens with an evocation of O'Connell's trial in 1843 and is markedly sympathetic, but *Castle Richmond*, reviewing the Famine in Munster, is more despairing and brutally providentialist in its implications.

66. 13 Aug. 1849, *Collected Letters*, Vol. XXIV (1995), p. 193.

67. *Selected Writings*, p. 172.

68. 1 Mar. 1847, *Collected Letters*, Vol. XXI (1993), p. 169.

69. Morrow, 'Thomas Carlyle, "Young Ireland" and the "Condition of Ireland Question"', pp. 643–67: Morrow persuasively argues that, illiberal and authoritarian as Carlyle's ideas on Ireland were, they were not based on racializing the Irish, but on universal failures in leadership and social morality.

70. *Nation*, 1 Sept. 1849; quoted in Morrow, 'Thomas Carlyle, "Young Ireland" and the "Condition of Ireland Question"', p. 663.

71. To Clarendon, 6 July 1849, *Collected Letters*, Vol. XXIV (1995), p. 104. To W. E. Forster he wrote, about Duffy (ibid., p. 144, 24 July 1849): 'From him I have seen the *wrong* or Catholic side of things all along, as from others I have amply enough seen what is represented as the *right* side. A very ugly bit of tapestry on whatever side seen! Nevertheless great seeds of improvement are visibly sown; the next generation of Irishmen may fairly hope to be ahead of any of its predecessors – nearer to a level with Englishmen than has ever been the case before.' Unsurprisingly, he believed this would not be brought about by laisser-faire economics and the Poor Law, but by 'that actual command of the Foolish Multitude by the Wise Few' (to Clarendon, 5 Aug. 1849, ibid., p. 173).

72. To Clarendon, 5 Aug. 1849, ibid, p. 173.

73. For Young Ireland in fiction see Fegan, *Literature and the Irish Famine*, pp. 226ff. An early instance is Marmion Savage's *The Falcon Family; or, Young Ireland* (1845); Pigot is lampooned as 'Tighearnan MacMorris', whose life is devoted to bringing Stonehenge 'back' to Ireland.

74. For Duffy and Parnell see R. Barry O'Brien, *The Life of Charles Stewart Parnell 1846–1891* (2 vols., London, 1898), Vol. I, p. 77, and Vol. II, pp. 56–95 (Duffy's own account of his relations with Parnell). For the 1875 election, also see Duffy to George Petrie [n.d., but 1875], NLI MS 5758, fols. 31–4, complaining that his candidature had been

killed off by a caucus involving the Dillons. 'I know nothing of Mr Parnell, except that he is reported to be a young man of good character and position.'

75. For the remarkably nationalist speech of Butt defending Smith O'Brien and the 'Traversers' see *Nation*, 20 May 1848: it emphasizes the betrayal of the Union by Britain, and the anti-Irish prejudices of the English, and was greatly applauded by nationalist Ireland. It should be connected to the Protestant Repeal 'moment'. Also see Joseph Spence, 'Isaac Butt, Irish Nationality and the Conditional Defence of the Union 1833–1870' in D. George Boyce and Alan O'Day (eds.), *Defenders of the Union: A Survey of British and Irish Unionism since 1801* (London, 2001), pp. 65–89.

76. Other writings of Butt's at this time seemed to imply the treatment of Ireland as a separate state (Spence, 'The Philosophy of Irish Toryism 1833–1852', pp. 261–2, 264), while Mitchel thought Butt's political economy lectures at Trinity constituted admirable manifestos for Repeal; the same might be said of Butt's 1847 Famine pamphlet, *A Voice for Ireland*.

77. *Nation*, 25 Mar. 1843. The writer does admit that both these 'provinces resolved to be nations' must first engineer unity within their borders.

78. T. F. Meagher, *Speeches on the Legislative Independence of Ireland, with Introductory Notes* (New York, 1853), p. 4.

79. 'Coole Park and Ballylee, 1931', Allt and Alspach (eds.), *The Variorum Edition of the Poems of W. B. Yeats*, pp. 491–2.

80. *Essays and Introductions* (London, 1961), p. 510.

3 Lost in the Big House: Anglo-Irishry and the Uses of the Supernatural

1. Lord Dunsany, *The Curse of the Wise Woman* (London, 1933), pp. 14–15.

2. Ibid., p. 10.

3. For their relationship see my *Apprentice Mage* and *W. B. Yeats: A Life. Vol. II: The Arch-Poet 1915–1939* (Oxford, 2003). Dunsany came to believe that Yeats and Gregory plagiarized his work, while Yeats complained of Dunsany's rudeness to him.

4. For a perceptive treatment of the Big House novel and its relation to women's writing, see Ó Gallchoir, *Maria Edgeworth*, pp. 176–80.

5. See Victor Sage, *Horror Fiction in the Protestant Tradition* (London, 1988) and his introductions to the Penguin Classic editions of *Melmoth the Wanderer* (2001) and *Uncle Silas* (2000). Gibbons, *Gaelic Gothic*, pp. 57ff., makes suggestive points about the part played by both Irish Catholicism and Puritan fanaticism in the construction of Irish Gothic fiction.

6. Spence, 'The Philosophy of Irish Toryism 1833–1852', p. 127.

7. As suggested in 'The Story of Ireland' in my *The Irish Story*, pp. 1–22. For other treatments of the supposed connection see Bhabha (ed.), *Nation and Narration*.

8. See Trumpener, *Bardic Nationalism*, pp. 249ff.

9. As did B. M. Croker and Frances Cashel Hoey: a point I owe to Claire Connolly. Also see S. B. Cook, 'The Irish Raj: Social Origins and Careers of Irishmen in the Indian Civil Service, *Journal of Social History*, 20, 3 (1987), and *Imperial Affinities: Nineteenth-Century Analogies and Exchanges between India and Ireland* (Delhi, 1993); Kevin Kenny, *Ireland and the British Empire* (Oxford, 2006); C. A. Bayly, 'Ireland, India and the Empire 1780–1914' in *Transactions of the Royal Historical Society*, sixth series, Vol. X (Cambridge, 2000); Barry Crosbie, 'The Irish Expatriate Community in British India *c.* 1750–1900' (Ph.D., Cambridge, 2004); D. H. Akenson, *If the Irish Ran the World: Montserrat 1630–1730* (Liverpool, 1997); Stephen Howe, *Ireland and Empire: Colonial Legacies in Irish History and Culture* (Oxford, 2000), especially Chapter 4.

10. In the 1920s he wanted Norah McGuinness to illustrate Le Fanu's *In a Glass Darkly*: see Yeats to Mrs Phibbs [McGuinness], 15 June 1925, *Collected Letters* (InteLex edition), accession no. 4739.

11. *Handbook of Political Fallacies*, quoted in Dwan, *The Great Community*, p. 160.

12. For a useful treatment see Damien Murray, *Romanticism, Nationalism and Irish Antiquarian Societies 1840–1880* (Maynooth, 2000).

13. T. C. Croker, *Fairy Legends and Traditions of the South of Ireland*, Vol. I (London, 1825), pp. 362–3.

14. See Sinéad Garrigan Mattar's highly suggestive study, *Primitivism, Science and the Irish Revival* (Oxford, 2004), pp. 2ff., 6, 14; also, for Yeats and academic Celtologists, pp. 36–7.

15. 'Protestant Magic: W. B. Yeats and the Spell of Irish History', pp. 251–2 (*Paddy and Mr Punch*, p. 220).

16. See, *inter alia*, Gibbons, *Gaelic Gothic*; Eagleton, *Heathcliff and the Great Hunger*; Killeen, *Gothic Ireland*; W. J. McCormack, 'Irish Gothic and After 1820–1945' in Deane, Carpenter, and Williams (eds.), *The Field Day Anthology*, Vol. II, pp. 831–54; Selina Guinness, '"Protestant Magic" Reappraised: Evangelicalism, Dissent and Theosophy' in *Irish University Review* (Spring/Summer 2003), pp. 14–27.

17. Which is actually *droch-fhuil*. One mischievous reviewer suggested that a better reading might be *droch-ollamh*, 'bad professor': Nicholas Daly in *Irish University Review*, 33, 1 (Spring/Summer 2003), pp. 227–9. The work in question is Joseph Valente, *Dracula's Crypt: Bram Stoker, Irishness and the Question of Blood* (Chicago, 2002).

18. David Lloyd, afterword in Belanger (ed.), *The Irish Novel in the Nineteenth Century*, p. 233, and Deane, *Strange Country*, pp. 91ff., 106, 119. For a more sceptical version see David Glover, *Vampires, Mummies and Liberals: Bram Stoker and the Politics of Popular Fiction* (London, 1996), Chapter 1.

19. See Clive Leatherdale, *The Origins of 'Dracula': The Background to Bram Stoker's Gothic Masterpiece* (London, 1987).

20. A possibility emphasized by Paul Murray, *From the Shadow of Dracula: A Life of Bram Stoker* (London, 2004), pp. 191, 194–5. See ibid., pp.181ff., for Stoker's other reading.

21. Eagleton, *Heathcliff and the Great Hunger*, pp. 215–16. For more convincing uses of *Dracula*, see Glover, *Vampires, Mummies and Liberals*, and Elaine Showalter, *Sexual Anarchy: Gender and Culture at the Fin de Siècle* (London, 1991), pp. 179–84.

22. See Murray, *From the Shadow of Dracula*, p. 61, for previous vampire appearances and a possible Le Fanu connection. George Moore was also using vampire imagery in the 1870s, perhaps derived from Baudelaire. Also see Gibbons, *Gaelic Gothic*, Chapter 8. For Carleton see Fegan, *Literature and the Irish Famine*, pp. 158–9.

23. W. S. Le Fanu, *Uncle Silas*, Victor Sage (ed.) (Penguin Classic edition, London, 2000), p. 444. The Swedenborgian Dr Bryerly turns out to be Maud's deliverer. For McCormack's reading see his valuable study *Sheridan Le Fanu and Victorian Ireland*, pp. 149–94.

24. 'Uncle Silas by Sheridan Le Fanu: Introduction to the Cresset Press Edition' in *The Mulberry Tree: Writings of Elizabeth Bowen*, selected and introduced by Hermione Lee (London, 1986), p. 101.

25. Pittock, *Scottish and Irish Romanticism*, p. 212.

26. Robert Tracy, *The Unappeasable Host: Studies in Irish Identities* (Dublin, 1998), p. 62.

27. W. R. Le Fanu, *Seventy Years of Irish Life, being Anecdotes and Reminiscences* (London, 1893), p. 59.

28. See Christopher Morash, *Writing the Irish Famine* (Oxford, 1995), pp. 134–42.

29. V. S. Pritchett, *The Living Novel* (London, 1946), p. 96.

30. See my essay ' "Now Shall I Make My Soul": Approaching Death in Yeats's Life and Work', *Proceedings of the British Academy*, 151 (Oxford, 2007), pp. 350–1.

31. Ian D'Alton has established this vividly for Cork Protestants in 'Survival! Some Reflections on Cork Protestant Families in the Nineteenth and Twentieth Centuries', *Irish Genealogist*, 11, 1 (2002), pp. 20–30, and in his M.A. thesis 'Southern Irish Unionism: A

Study of Cork City and County Unionists 1885–1914' (University College, Cork, 1972).

32. Key texts might include Stephen Gwynn, *Experiences of a Literary Man* (London, 1926), Elizabeth Bowen, *'Bowen's Court' and 'Seven Winters'* (London and Dublin, 1942), and William Magan, *Umma-More: The Story of an Irish Family* (Salisbury, 1983).

33. W. Y. Evans-Wentz, *The Fairy-Faith in Celtic Countries* (Oxford, 1911), *passim*; see p. 30, for Hyde's views on ancient inheritors.

34. The most recent edition is by New York Review Book Classics (2007), with an illuminating introduction by Marina Warner.

35. On fallen-angel theories see W. B. Yeats, *Mythologies*, Warwick Gould and Deirdre Toomey (eds.) (London, 2005), p. 239, fn. 6: Yeats and William Wilde both give Irish sources for this belief, as does Augusta Gregory in *Visions and Beliefs in the West of Ireland* (2 vols., London, 1920), Vol. I, pp. 212–14.

36. Murray, *Romanticism, Nationalism and Irish Antiquarian Societies*, p. 111; Evans-Wentz, *The Fairy-Faith in Celtic Countries*, pp. 284ff., 335.

37. Evans-Wentz, *The Fairy-Faith in Celtic Countries*, pp. 232, 466ff.

38. *The Burning of Bridget Cleary* (London, 1999), p. 29.

39. Evans-Wentz, *The Fairy-Faith in Celtic Countries*, pp. 46, 71.

40. Fegan, *Literature and the Irish Famine*, pp. 165–6, 177–80.

41. Lady Wilde, *Ancient Cures, Charms and Usages of Ireland* (London, 1890), p. 1. For Lady Wilde and Swedenborg see Joy Melville, *Mother of Oscar: The Life of Jane Francesca Wilde* (London, 1994), p. 59. James Hyde's *A Bibliography of the Works of Emmanuel Swedenborg* (London, 1906) describes the 1853 edition of *The Future Life* as a version of *Concerning Heaven and Its Wonders, and Concerning Hell* 'revised, as it appears, by "Speranza", Lady Wilde'. However, in 'Additional Notes and Corrections' he retracts this, adding that 'the edition was not revised by Lady Wilde, but by John Simms, its publisher.' My thanks to James Wilson for this reference.

42. See Fegan, *Literature and the Irish Famine*, pp. 150, 158, for Carleton's use of biblical imagery.

43. *English Literature in Our Time and the University*, p. 137.

44. See *The Arch-Poet*, pp. 618–20, 627–9. He told the Abbey audience: 'I wish to say that I have put into this play not many thoughts that are picturesque, but my own beliefs about this world and the next.'

45. W. B. Yeats, *Mythologies*, Gould and Toomey (eds.), p. 368. For a discussion of his redrafting of this key passage see *The Arch-Poet*, p. 79.

4 Oisin Comes Home: Yeats as Inheritor

1. Richard Ellmann, *Eminent Domain*, p. 3.

2. J. M. Hone, *W. B. Yeats 1865–1939* (revised edition, London, 1962), p. 46.

3. I owe this insight to the research of Eamonn Cantwell, ' "To Write for My Own Race": The Irish Response to W. B. Yeats in His Lifetime' (Ph.D., Trinity College Dublin, 2002), pp. 31–5.

4. *Irish Fireside*, 9 Oct. 1886, reprinted in Frayne (ed.), *Uncollected Prose*, Vol. I, pp. 81–7.

5. Jug Mohit Chaudhury, *Yeats, the Irish Literary Revival and the Politics of Print* (Cork, 2001), p. 12.

6. The footnotes of Douglas Hyde's folktale collection *Beside the Fire: A Collection of Irish Gaelic Folk Stories* (London, 1910 edition) include suggestive references to Theosophists like Colonel Olcott visiting Dublin (see p. 190); and Yeats was introduced to Esoteric Buddhism by his aunt Isabella Varley.

7. For the production and reception of this volume see my *Apprentice Mage*, pp. 148–52.

8. Ibid., pp. 17, 24. *Rob Roy* also remained in his mind, to judge by WBY's use of 'Diana Vernon' as a sobriquet for Olivia Shakespear in his *Memoirs*. Other echoes include the phrase 'the iron time' (which he would have heard in the introduction to the *Lay*), and the phrase

'hysterica passio' (for Scott's use of it see A. N. Wilson, *The Laird of Abbotsford: A View of Sir Walter Scott* (London, 1980), p. 64). (Both probably derive the last from *Lear*, II.4.)

9. Frayne (ed.), *Uncollected Prose*, Vol. I, p. 35.

10. George Bornstein, *Yeats and Shelley* (Chicago, 1970); Warwick Gould and Deirdre Toomey's introduction and notes to their edition of W. B. Yeats, *Mythologies*; Mary Helen Thuente, *W. B. Yeats and Irish Folklore* (Dublin, 1980); Matthew Campbell, 'Poetry in English 1830–1890' in Kelleher and O'Leary (eds.), *The Cambridge History of Irish Literature*, Vol. I, pp. 534–8; Marcus, *Yeats and the Beginning of the Irish Literary Renaissance*.

11. Kelly (ed.) with Domvile, *The Collected Letters of W. B. Yeats*, Vol. I, p. 176. Also see Russell K. Alspach, 'Some Sources of W. B. Yeats's "The Wanderings of Oisin"', *PMLA*, 58 (Sept. 1943), pp. 849–66.

12. *Autobiographies* (London, 1966), p. 189.

13. Samuel Ferguson, *Lays of the Western Gael* (Dublin, 1888), p. 156.

14. Allt and Alspach (eds.), *The Variorum Edition of the Poems of W. B. Yeats*, pp. 121–2.

15. *DUR*, Jan. and Mar. 1886 for Oldham and Gregg; June 1886 for Oldham on 'The Prospects of Irish Nationality'; May 1886 for Chatterjee and Davis. See also Chaudhury, *Yeats, the Irish Literary Revival and the Politics of Print*, pp. 59ff. Ferguson also was an off-stage presence in Yeats's own life; the Fergusons lived, in considerably grander circumstances, near the Yeatses in Howth, after JBY took his family back to Dublin in 1881.

16. See Chaudhury, *Yeats, the Irish Literary Revival and the Politics of Print*, pp. 35ff.

17. *Beside the Fire*, p. xliii.

18. To Olivia Shakespear, 30 June 1932, *Collected Letters* (InteLex electronic edition), accession number 5692; also in Allan Wade (ed.), *The Letters of W. B. Yeats* (London, 1954), p. 798.

19. Frayne (ed.), *Uncollected Prose*, Vol. I, pp. 47ff., for a relevant commentary on Yeats and mythology. Also see Murray, *Romanticism, Nationalism and Irish Antiquarian Societies*, pp. 32–3, 56–7, 75ff.

20. Preface to Lady Gregory's *Cuchulain of Muirthemne* (1902), reprinted in *Prefaces and Introductions: Uncollected Prefaces and Introductions by Yeats to Works by Other Authors and to Anthologies Edited by Yeats*, William O'Donnell (ed.) (London, 1988), p. 124.

21. Allt and Alspach (eds.), *The Variorum Edition of the Poems of W. B. Yeats*, p. 138.

22. *Apprentice Mage*, p. 53.

23. M. J. Kelly, *The Fenian Ideal and Irish Nationalism*, p. 34.

24. Ibid., pp. 17, 22–40.

25. *Irish Literary Gazette*, Mar. 1899, quoted in Warwick Gould (ed.), 'Lionel Johnson's "The Ideal of Thomas Davis" (1896)' in *Yeats Annual No. 14: Yeats and the Nineties* (London, 2001), p. 107. Yeats's defence, in a letter to the *Freeman's Journal*, is in Warwick Gould, John Kelly, and Deirdre Toomey (eds.), *The Collected Letters of W. B. Yeats. Vol. II: 1896–1900* (Oxford, 1997), pp. 387–8. But he had already called 'Fontenoy' 'a savourless imitation of Macaulay' in a review attacking Duffy's Library of Ireland publications in June 1896: Frayne (ed.), *Uncollected Prose*, Vol. I, p. 408.

26. 'The one excellent thing, the one seasonable thing, that cried out to be done': *Bookman* review of Duffy's *Young Ireland*, reprinted in John P. Frayne and Colton Johnson, *Uncollected Prose by W. B. Yeats. Vol. II: Reviews, Articles and Other Miscellaneous Prose 1897–1939* (London, 1975), p. 35.

27. W. B. Yeats, *Tribute to Thomas Davis* (Cork, 1965).

28. Chaudhury, *Yeats, the Irish Literary Revival and the Politics of Print*, p. 73, for Davis cult and pp. 220ff. for the politics of adopting Davis, Mangan, and Ferguson.

29. *Autobiographies*, pp. 224–5.

30. For Yeats's politics in this era see Deirdre Toomey's magisterial essay 'Who Fears to Speak of Ninety-Eight?' in Gould (ed.), *Yeats Annual No. 14*, pp. 209–61. Also *Apprentice Mage*, Chapter 5.

31. W. B. Yeats, *Memoirs*, Denis Donoghue (ed.) (London, 1972; 1988 edition), pp. 250–1.

32. This piece of juvenilia is in *Manuscript Materials by W. B. Yeats: The Early Poetry. Vol. II: 'The Wanderings of Oisin' and Other Early Poems to 1895*, George Bornstein (ed.) (London and Ithaca, 1994); first published with a commentary by Christina Hunt Mahony and Edward O'Shea in *Poetry*, 135 (Jan. 1980), it is also to be found in W. B. Yeats, *Under the Moon: The Unpublished Early Poetry*, George Bornstein (ed.) (New York, 1995), p. 93.

33. See my essay 'Square Built Power and Fiery Shorthand: Yeats, Carleton and the Irish Nineteenth Century' in *The Irish Story*, pp. 95–112. For a contrasting view of what Yeats saw in Carleton see Emer Nolan, *Catholic Emancipations*, pp. 96–101.

34. See Margaret Kelleher, ' "Wanted, an Irish Novelist": The Critical Decline of the Nineteenth-Century Irish Novel' in Belanger (ed.), *The Irish Novel in the Nineteenth Century*, p. 193.

35. Kelly (ed.) with Domvile, *The Collected Letters of W. B. Yeats*, Vol. I, pp. 198–200.

36. For example, Kelleher, ' "Wanted, an Irish Novelist" ', p. 198.

37. 2 Dec. 1891, Gould, Kelly, and Toomey (eds.), *The Collected Letters of W. B. Yeats*, Vol. II, p. 275.

38. W. B. Yeats, *Prefaces and Introductions*, William O'Donnell (ed.), p. 37.

39. See Chaudhury, *Yeats, the Irish Literary Revival and the Politics of Print*, p. 203.

40. *Apprentice Mage*, pp. 117–24.

41. Ibid., pp. 145ff.

42. See Kelleher, ' "Wanted, an Irish Novelist" ', pp. 187ff., and also her valuable article 'The Cabinet of Irish Literature: A Historical Perspective on Irish Anthologies', Éire-Ireland, 38 (Winter 2003), pp. 68–89.

43. Kelly (ed.) with Domvile, The Collected Letters of W. B. Yeats, Vol. I, pp. 430–31.

44. Frayne (ed.), Uncollected Prose, Vol. I, p. 385.

45. Kelly (ed.) with Domvile, The Collected Letters of W. B. Yeats, Vol. I, p. 442.

46. The notes to Fairy and Folk Tales also bear witness to the politics of the Young Ireland societies and the Contemporary Club: 'Many in Ireland consider Sir Samuel Ferguson their greatest poet. The English reader will most likely never have heard his name, for Anglo-Irish critics, who have found an English audience, being more Anglo than Irish, have been content to follow English opinion instead of leading it, in all matters concerning Ireland.' Fairy and Folk Tales of the Irish Peasantry (London and New York, 1888), p. 320.

47. Sinéad Garrigan Mattar, Primitivism, Science, and the Irish Revival (Oxford, 2004), pp. 44ff.

48. Yeats's enthusiasm for this story is repeatedly expressed in Kelly (ed.) with Domvile, The Collected Letters of W. B. Yeats, Vol. I, pp. 88–9, 112, 182, 229, 441.

49. Yeats delightedly retailed this in his 1890 review of Ancient Cures, Charms and Usages of Ireland (Frayne (ed.), Uncollected Prose, Vol. I, p. 171).

50. In an inscription in a copy of his Stories from Carleton, to John Quinn: Allan Wade, A Bibliography of the Writings of W. B. Yeats (London, 1958), p. 220.

51. Conrad M. Arensberg, The Irish Countryman: An Anthropological Study (London, 1937), p. 214; also see Chapter 6, passim.

52. W. B. Yeats, Mythologies, Gould and Toomey (eds.), p. 61.

53. E. J. Hobsbawm and T. O. Ranger (eds.), The Invention of Tradition (Oxford, 1983).

54. *Explorations*, p. 30.

55. Thuente, *W. B. Yeats and Irish Folklore*, pp. 152–3.

56. For guidance through this tangled web see W. B. Yeats, *Mythologies*, Gould and Toomey (eds.), and *The Secret Rose: Stories by W. B. Yeats. A Variorum Edition*, Warwick Gould, Phillip L. Marcus, and Michael J. Sidnell (eds.) (second edition, revised and enlarged, London, 1992).

57. See Donald Masterson and Edward O'Shea, 'Code Breaking and Myth Making: The Ellis–Yeats Edition of Blake's Works' in Warwick Gould (ed.), *Yeats Annual No. 3* (London, 1985), pp. 53–80.

58. Principally John O'Daly and Edward Walsh, *Reliques of Irish Jacobite Poetry* (1844), Walsh, *Irish Popular Songs* (1847), and Mangan's *Poets and Poetry of Munster* (1849): see Thuente, *W. B. Yeats and Irish Folklore*, p. 198.

59. See the frontispiece to my *Apprentice Mage*, p. xxiv.

60. 30 May 1897, Gould, Kelly, and Toomey (eds.), *The Collected Letters of W. B. Yeats*, Vol. II, p. 104.

61. W. B. Yeats, *Mythologies*, Gould and Toomey (eds.), p. 91.

62. Frayne (ed.), *Uncollected Prose*, Vol. I, pp. 266–75.

63. Ibid., p. 269.

64. Allt and Alspach (eds.), *The Variorum Edition of the Poems of W. B. Yeats*, p. 446.

65. Frayne (ed.), *Uncollected Prose*, Vol. I, p. 273. For a perceptive analysis see Marcus, *Yeats and the Beginning of the Irish Literary Renaissance*, pp. 17–19.

66. NLI MS 3726A. The cover is photographed in Bornstein (ed.), *Manuscript Materials by W. B. Yeats: The Early Poetry. Vol. II*, p. 28.

WORKS CITED AND CONSULTED

Primary Sources

Works by Yeats

Fairy and Folk Tales of the Irish Peasantry (London, 1888)

Representative Irish Tales (Boston, 1891, reprint with an introduction by Mary-Helen Thuente, Gerrards Cross, 1979)

Essays and Introductions (London, 1961)

Explorations (London, 1962)

Tribute to Thomas Davis (Cork, 1965)

Autobiographies (London, 1966)

The Variorum Edition of the Poems of W. B. Yeats, Peter Allt and Russell K. Alspach (eds.) (third printing, New York, 1966)

Uncollected Prose by W. B. Yeats. Vol. I: First Reviews and Articles 1886–1896, John P. Frayne (ed.) (London, 1970)

Memoirs, Denis Donoghue (ed.) (London, 1972)

Uncollected Prose by W. B. Yeats. Vol. II: Reviews, Articles and Other Miscellaneous Prose 1897–1939, John P. Frayne and Colton Johnson (eds.) (London, 1975)

Prefaces and Introductions: Uncollected Prefaces and Introductions by Yeats to Works by Other Authors and to Anthologies Edited by Yeats, William O'Donnell (ed.) (London, 1988)

Letters to the New Island: A New Edition, George Bornstein and Hugh Witemayer (eds.), (London, 1989)

The Secret Rose: Stories by W. B. Yeats. A Variorum Edition, Warwick Gould, Phillip L. Marcus, and Michael J. Sidnell (eds.) (second edition, revised and enlarged, London, 1992)

Manuscript Materials by W. B. Yeats: The Early Poetry. Vol. II: 'The Wanderings of Oisin' and Other Early Poems to 1895, George Bornstein (ed.) (London and Ithaca, 1994)

Under the Moon: The Unpublished Early Poetry, George Bornstein (ed.) (New York, 1995)

Mythologies, Warwick Gould and Deirdre Toomey (eds.) (London, 2005)

Works by others

Banim, John, *The Boyne Water* ([1826], reprint Bernard Escarbelt (ed.), CERIUL Anglo-Irish Texts, Patrick Rafroidi (ed.), Lille, 1976)

—— *The Nawlans* ([1826], reprint Kevin Casey (ed.), Belfast, 2004)

Carlyle, Thomas, *Selected Writings*, Alan Shelston (ed.) (Harmondsworth, 1971)

Croker, Thomas Crofton, *Fairy Legends and Traditions of the South of Ireland* (London, 1825)

Davis, Thomas, *The Poems of Thomas Davis: Now First Collected, with Notes and Historical Illustrations* [Thomas Wallis (ed.)] (Dublin, 1846)

Deane, Seamus, Carpenter, Andrew, and Williams, Jonathan (eds.), *The Field Day Anthology of Irish Writing* (Vols. I–III, Derry, 1991); Angela Bourke *et al.* (eds.), (Vols. IV–V, Cork, 2002)

Dunsany, Lord, *The Curse of the Wise Woman* (London, 1933)

Edgeworth, Maria, *Castle Rackrent* ([1800], and *Ennui* [1809], reprint Marilyn Butler (ed.), Harmondsworth, 1992)

—— *The Absentee* ([1812], reprint Heidi Thomson (ed.), London, 2000)

—— *Ormond* ([1817], reprint Claire Connolly (ed.), London, 2000)

Ferguson, Lady [Mary], *Sir Samuel Ferguson in the Ireland of His Day* (2 vols., London, 1896)

Ferguson, Samuel, *Lays of the Western Gael* (Dublin, 1888)

Gould, Warwick (ed.), 'Lionel Johnson's "The Ideal of Thomas Davis" (1896)' in *Yeats Annual No. 14: Yeats and the Nineties* (London, 2001)

Gregory, Lady [Augusta], *Visions and Beliefs in the West of Ireland* (2 vols., London, 1920)

Gwynn, Stephen, 'Novels of Irish Life in the Nineteenth Century' (1897, reprinted in *Irish Books and Irish People*, London, 1919)

Hogg, James, *The Private Memoirs and Confessions of a Justified Sinner* ([1824], reprint John Carey (ed.), Oxford, 1995)

Hyde, Douglas, *Beside the Fire: A Collection of Irish Gaelic Folk Stories* (London, 1890, 1910)

Kirk, Robert, *The Secret Commonwealth: An Essay on the Nature and Actions of the Subterranean (and for the Most Part Invisible) People Heretofore Going under the Name of Elves, Fauns and Fairies* ([1815, 1893], facsimile edition with an introduction by Marina Warner, New York, 2007)

Lecky, W. E. H., *History of Ireland in the Eighteenth Century* (5 vols., London, 1892)

Le Fanu, Joseph Sheridan, *Uncle Silas* ([1864], reprint Victor Sage (ed.), London 2000)

—— *In A Glass Darkly* ([1872], reprint Robert Tracy (ed.) Oxford, 1993)

Maddyn, D. O., *Ireland and Its Rulers* (3 vols., London, 1843–4)

Maturin, Charles, *Melmoth the Wanderer* ([1820], reprint Victor Sage (ed.), London, 2001)

Meagher, T. F., *Speeches on the Legislative Independence of Ireland, with Introductory Notes* (New York, 1853)

Moore, Thomas, *Memoirs of Captain Rock, the Celebrated Irish Chieftain, with Some Account of His Ancestors, Written by Himself* ([1824], reprint Seamus Deane and Emer Nolan (eds.), Dublin, 2009)

—— 'Irish Novels', *Edinburgh Review*, 43 (Feb. 1826), pp. 356–72

Nation, 1843–9

Owenson, Sydney, *The Wild Irish Girl* ([1806], reprint Claire Connolly and Stephen Copley (eds.), London, 2000)

Owenson, Sydney, *The O'Briens and the O'Flahertys: A National Tale* ([1827], reprint with an introduction by Mary Campbell, London, 1988)

Scott, Walter, *Waverley* ([1814], reprint Ian Duncan (ed.), Edinburgh, 2007)

—— *The Antiquary* ([1816], reprint Nicola J. Watson (ed.), Oxford, 2002)

—— *Redgauntlet* ([1824], reprint G. A. M. Wood (ed.), Edinburgh, 1997)

Stoker, Bram, *Dracula* ([1897], reprint Maurice Hindle (ed.), introduction by Christopher Frayling, London, 2003)

Trollope, Anthony, *The Kellys and the O'Kellys* ([1848], reprint W. J. McCormack, introduction by William Trevor, Oxford, 1992)

—— *Castle Richmond* ([1860], reprint Mary Hamer (ed.), Oxford, 1989)

Wilde, Lady [Jane Francesca], *Ancient Cures, Charms and Usages of Ireland* (London, 1890)

Contemporary Memoirs, Letters, and Diaries

Beaumont, Gustave de, *Ireland: Social, Political and Religious* ([1839], reprint W. C. Taylor (ed.), with an introduction by Tom Garvin and Andreas Hess, Cambridge, Mass., 2006)

Carlyle, Jane Welsh and Thomas, *Collected Letters of Thomas and Jane Welsh Carlyle*, Charles Richard Sanders, K. J. Fielding, Ian Campbell *et al.* (eds.) (Edinburgh and Durham, NC, 1970–)

—— *Newly Selected Letters*, Kenneth J. Fielding and David R. Sorensen (eds.) (Aldershot, 2004)

Duffy, Charles Gavan, *Young Ireland: A Fragment of Irish History 1840–1850* (London, 1880)

—— *Four Years of Irish History 1845–1849* (London, 1883)

—— *Conversations with Carlyle* (London, 1892)

—— *My Life in Two Hemispheres* (2 vols., London, 1903)

Gwynn, Stephen, *Experiences of a Literary Man* (London, 1926)

Le Fanu, W. R., *Seventy Years of Irish Life, being Anecdotes and Reminiscences* (London, 1893)

O'Brien, R. Barry, *The Life of Charles Stewart Parnell 1846–1891* (2 vols., London, 1898)

Scott, Walter, *Letters*, J. G. Grierson *et al.* (eds.) (12 vols., London, 1832–8)

—— *Sir Walter Scott's Tour in Ireland in 1825*, D. J. O'Donoghue (ed.) (Dublin, 1905)

Tocqueville, Alexis de, *Journeys to England and Ireland*, J. P. Mayer (ed.) (London, 1958)

Yeats, W. B., *Collected Letters*, InteLex electronic edition

—— *The Letters of W. B. Yeats*, Allan Wade (ed.) (London, 1954)

—— *W. B. Yeats: Interviews and Recollections*, E. H. Mikhail (ed.) (2 vols., London, 1977)

—— *The Collected Letters of W. B. Yeats. Vol. I: 1865–1895*, John Kelly (ed.) with Eric Domvile (Oxford, 1986)

—— *The Collected Letters of W. B. Yeats. Vol. II: 1896–1900*, Warwick Gould, John Kelly, and Deirdre Toomey (eds.) (Oxford, 1997)

Secondary Sources

Adams, J. R. R., *The Printed Word and the Common Man: Popular Culture in Ulster 1700–1900* (Belfast, 1997)

Akenson, D. H., *If the Irish Ran the World: Montserrat, 1630–1730* (Liverpool, 1997)

Alspach, Russell K., 'Some Sources of W. B. Yeats's "The Wanderings of Oisin"', *PMLA*, 58 (Sept. 1943), pp. 849–66

Anderson, Benedict, *Imagined Communities: Reflections on the Origin and Spread of Nationalism* (London, 1983)

——'Selective Kinship', *Dublin Review*, 10 (Spring 2003), pp. 5–29

Anderson, James, *Sir Walter Scott and History* (Edinburgh, 1981)

Andrews, J. H., *A Paper Landscape: The Ordnance Survey in Nineteenth-Century Ireland* (Oxford, 1975)

Arensberg, Conrad M., *The Irish Countryman: An Anthropological Study* (London, 1937)

Bayly, C. A., 'Ireland, India and the Empire 1780–1914', *Transactions of the Royal Historical Society*, sixth series, Vol. X (Cambridge, 2000)

Bew, John, *The Glory of Being Britons: Civic Unionism in Nineteenth-Century Belfast* (Dublin, 2008)

Black, R. D. Collison, *Economic Thought and the Irish Question 1817–1870* (Cambridge, 1960)

Bornstein, George, *Yeats and Shelley* (Chicago, 1970)

Bourke, Angela, *The Burning of Bridget Cleary* (London, 1999)

Bowen, Elizabeth, *'Bowen's Court' and 'Seven Winters'* (London and Dublin, 1942)

—— 'Uncle Silas by Sheridan Le Fanu: Introduction to the Cresset Press Edition' in *The Mulberry Tree: Writings of Elizabeth Bowen*, selected and introduced by Hermione Lee (London, 1986)

Brennan, Timothy, 'The National Longing for Form' in Homi K. Bhabha (ed.), *Nation and Narration* (London, 1990), pp. 44–70

Burgess, Miranda, 'The National Tale and Allied Genres 1770s–1840s' in J. W. Foster, *The Cambridge Companion to the Irish Novel* (Cambridge, 2006)

Butler, Marilyn, 'Irish Culture and Scottish Enlightenment: Maria Edgeworth's Histories of the Future' in Stefan Collini, Richard Whatmore, and Brian Young (eds.), *Economy, Polity and Society: British Intellectual History 1750–1950* (Cambridge, 2000), pp. 158–80

Brown, Malcolm, *The Politics of Irish Literature from Thomas Davis to W. B. Yeats* (London, 1972)

—— *Samuel Ferguson* (Lewisburg, Pa., 1973)

Cahalan, James M., *Great Hatred, Little Room: The Irish Historical Novel* (Dublin, 1983)

Campbell, Matthew, 'Poetry in English 1830–1890: From Catholic Emancipation to the Fall of Parnell' in Kelleher and O'Leary (eds.), *The
Cambridge History of Irish Literature* (Cambridge, 2006), pp. 504–15

Cantwell, Eamonn, '"To Write for My Own Race": The Irish Response
to W. B. Yeats in His Lifetime' (Ph.D., Trinity College Dublin, 2002)

Chaudhury, Jug Mohit, *Yeats, the Irish Literary Revival and the Politics of
Print* (Cork, 2001)

Cleary, Joe, 'The Nineteenth-Century Irish Novel: Notes and Speculations on Literary Historiography' in Jacqueline Belanger (ed.), *The
Irish Novel in the Nineteenth Century: Facts and Fictions* (Dublin, 2005)

Colley, Linda, *Britons: Forging the Nation 1707–1837* (London, 1992)

—— *Captives: British Empire and the World 1600–1850* (London, 2002)

—— *The Ordeal of Elizabeth Marsh* (London, 2007)

Connolly, Claire, 'Introduction: The Politics of Love in *The Wild Irish
Girl*' in Sydney Owenson, *The Wild Irish Girl*, Claire Connolly and
Stephen Copley (eds.) (London, 2000)

—— '"I Accuse Miss Owenson": *The Wild Irish Girl* as Media Event',
Colby Quarterly, 36, 2 (June 2000), pp. 98–115

—— 'Irish Romanticism 1800–1829' in Margaret Kelleher and Philip
O'Leary (eds.), *The Cambridge History of Irish Literature* (Cambridge,
2006)

—— 'Theater and Nation in Irish Romanticism: The Tragic Dramas of
Charles Robert Maturin and Richard Lalor Sheil', *Éire-Ireland*, 41, 3–4
(Fall/Winter 2006), pp. 185–214

Cook, S. B., 'The Irish Raj: Social Origins and Careers of Irishmen in
the Indian Civil Service, *Journal of Social History*, 20, 3 (1987)

—— *Imperial Affinities: Nineteenth-Century Analogies and Exchanges between
India and Ireland* (Delhi, 1993)

Corbett, Mary Jean, *Allegories of Union in Irish and English Writing 1790–1870:
Politics, History and the Family from Edgeworth to Arnold* (Cambridge, 2000)

Crawford, Robert, *Scotland's Books* (London, 2007)

Cronin, John, *Gerald Griffin 1803–1840: A Critical Biography* (Cambridge, 1978)

—— *The Anglo-Irish Novel. Vol. I: The Nineteenth Century* (Belfast, 1980)

Crosbie, Barry, 'The Irish Expatriate Community in British India *c.* 1750–1900' (Ph.D., Cambridge, 2004)

Curtis, L. P., *Apes and Angels: The Irishman in Victorian Caricature* (revised edition, Washington, DC, 1997)

D'Alton, Ian, 'Southern Irish Unionism: A Study of Cork City and County Unionists 1885–1914' (M.A., University College Cork, 1972)

—— 'Survival! Some Reflections on Cork Protestant Families in the Nineteenth and Twentieth Centuries', *Irish Genealogist*, 9, 1 (2002), pp. 20–30

D'Arcy, Julia Meldon, *Subversive Scott: The Waverley Novels and Scottish Nationalism* (Reykjavik, 2005)

Deane, Seamus, 'Irish National Character 1790–1900' in Tom Dunne (ed.), *The Writer as Witness: Literature as Historical Evidence*, Historical Studies XVI (Cork, 1987)

—— *Strange Country: Modernity and Nationhood in Irish Writing since 1790* (Oxford, 1997)

Dugger, Julie M., 'Black Ireland's Race: Thomas Carlyle and the Young Ireland Movement', *Victorian Studies*, 48, 3 (Spring 2006), pp. 461–85

Duncan, Ian, 'Ireland, Scotland and the Materials of Romanticism' in David Duff and Catherine Jones (eds.), *Scotland, Ireland and the Romantic Aesthetic* (Lewisburg, Pa., 2007), pp. 258–78

—— *Scott's Shadow: The Novel in Romantic Edinburgh* (Princeton, 2007)

Dunne, Tom, *Maria Edgeworth and the Colonial Mind* (Cork, 1984)

—— 'Haunted by History: Irish Romantic Writing 1800–1850' in R. Porter and M. Teich (eds.), *Romanticism in National Context* (Cambridge, 1988), pp. 68–91

—— ' "A Gentleman's Estate Should Be a Moral School": Edgeworthstown in Fact and Fiction 1780–1840' in Raymond Gillespie and Gerard Moran (eds.), *Longford: Essays in County History* (Dublin, 1991), pp. 95–121

—— 'Chivalry, the Harp and Maclise's Contribution to the Creation of National Identity' in Peter Murray (ed.), *Daniel Maclise 1806–1870: Romancing the Past* (Kinsale, 2008)

—— (ed.), *The Writer as Witness: Literature as Historical Evidence*, Historical Studies XVI (Cork, 1987)

Dwan, David, *The Great Community: Culture and Nationalism in Ireland* (Dublin, 2008)

Eagleton, Terry, *Heathcliff and the Great Hunger: Studies in Irish Culture* (London, 1995)

—— *Scholars and Rebels in Nineteenth-Century Ireland* (Oxford, 2000)

Edwards, Owen Dudley, '"True Thomas": Carlyle, Young Ireland and the Legacy of Millennialism' in David Sorensen and Rodger L. Tarr (eds.), *The Carlyles at Home and Abroad* (Aldershot, 2006), pp. 61–76

Eliot, T. S., 'The Poetry of W. B. Yeats', reprinted in J. Hall and Michael Steinman (eds.), *The Permanence of Yeats* (New York, 1950)

Ellmann, Richard, *Eminent Domain: Yeats among Wilde, Joyce, Pound, Eliot and Auden* (Oxford, 1967)

Fegan, Melissa, *Literature and the Irish Famine 1845–1919* (Oxford, 2002)

Ferris, Ina, *The Romantic National Tale and the Question of Ireland* (Cambridge, 2002)

Flanagan, Thomas, *The Irish Novelists* (London, 1959)

Foster, John Wilson (ed.), *The Cambridge Companion to the Irish Novel* (Cambridge, 2006)

—— *Irish Novels 1890–1940: New Bearings in Culture and Fiction* (Oxford, 2008)

Foster, R. F., 'Protestant Magic: W. B. Yeats and the Spell of Irish History' in *Proceedings of the British Academy*, 75 (1989), pp. 243–66, reprinted in *Paddy and Mr Punch: Connections in Irish and English History* (London, 1993), pp. 212–32

—— *W. B. Yeats: A Life. Vol. I: The Apprentice Mage 1865–1914* (Oxford, 1997)

—— *The Irish Story: Telling Tales and Making It Up in Ireland* (London, 2001)

—— *W. B. Yeats: A Life. Vol. II: The Arch-Poet 1915–1939* (Oxford, 2003)

—— ' "Now Shall I Make My Soul": Approaching Death in Yeats's Life and Work', *Proceedings of the British Academy*, 151 (Oxford, 2007), pp. 339–60

Garside, Peter, 'Popular Fiction and National Tale: Hidden Origins of Scott's *Waverley*', *Nineteenth-Century Literature*, 46, 1 (June 1991)

Gibbons, Luke, *Gaelic Gothic: Race, Colonization and Irish Culture* (Syracuse, 2006)

Glover, David, *Vampires, Mummies and Liberals: Bram Stoker and the Politics of Popular Fiction* (London, 1996)

Gray, Peter, *Famine, Land and Politics: British Government and Irish Society 1843–1850* (Dublin, 1999)

Guinness, Selina, ' "Protestant Magic" Reappraised: Evangelicalism, Dissent and Theosophy' in *Irish University Review* (Spring/Summer 2003), pp. 14–27

Hearne, John M., and Cornish, Rory T. (eds.), *Thomas Francis Meagher: The Making of an Irish-American* (Dublin, 2006)

Hobsbawm, E. J., and Ranger T. O. (eds.), *The Invention of Tradition* (Oxford, 1983)

Hone, J. M., *W. B. Yeats 1865–1939* (revised edition, London, 1962)

Howe, Stephen, *Ireland and Empire: Colonial Legacies in Irish History and Culture* (Oxford, 2000)

Kaplan, Cora, 'White, Black and Green: Racializing Irishness in Victorian England' in Peter Gray (ed.), *Victoria's Ireland? Irishness and Britishness 1837–1900* (Dublin, 2004)

Kelleher, Margaret, '*The Cabinet of Irish Literature*: A Historical Perspective on Irish Anthologies', *Éire-Ireland*, 38 (Winter 2003), pp. 68–89

—— ' "Wanted, an Irish Novelist": The Critical Decline of the Nineteenth-Century Irish Novel' in Jacqueline Belanger (ed.), *The Irish Novel in the Nineteenth Century: Facts and Fictions* (Dublin, 2005)

Kelly, Matthew, *The Fenian Ideal and Irish Nationalism 1882–1916* (Woodbridge, 2006)

Kelly, Ronan, *Bard of Erin: The Life of Thomas Moore* (Dublin, 2008)

Kenny, Kevin, *Ireland and the British Empire* (Oxford, 2006)

Kidd, Colin, *Subverting Scotland's Past: Whig Historians and the Creation of an Anglo-British Identity 1698–1830* (Cambridge, 1993)

—— *British Identities Before Nationalism: Ethnicity and Nationhood in the Atlantic World 1600–1900* (Cambridge, 1999)

Killeen, Jarlath, *Gothic Ireland: Horror and the Irish Anglican Imagination in the Long Eighteenth Century* (Dublin, 2005)

Leatherdale, Clive, *The Origins of 'Dracula': The Background to Bram Stoker's Gothic Masterpiece* (London, 1987)

Leavis, F. R., *English Literature in Our Time and the University* (London, 1969)

Leerssen, Joep, *Remembrance and Imagination: Patterns in the Historical and Literary Representation of Ireland in the Nineteenth Century* (Cork, 1997)

—— and Beller, Manfred (eds.), *Imagology: The Cultural Construction and Literary Representation of National Character – A Critical Survey* (Amsterdam, 2007)

Loeber, Rolf, 'Literary Absentees: Irish Women Writers in Nineteenth-Century England' in Jacqueline Belanger (ed.), *The Irish Novel in the Nineteenth Century: Facts and Fictions* (Dublin, 2005)

—— and Loeber-Stouthammer, Magda, with Burnham, Anne M., *A Guide to Irish Fiction 1650–1900* (Dublin, 2006)

McCaw, Neil (ed.), *Writing Irishness in Nineteenth-Century British Culture* (Aldershot, 2004)

McCormack, W. J., *Sheridan Le Fanu and Victorian Ireland* (Oxford, 1980)

—— *Ascendancy and Tradition in Anglo-Irish Literary History from 1789 to 1939* (Oxford, 1985)

McMaster, Graham, *Scott and Society* (Cambridge, 1981)

MacQueen, John, *The Rise of the Historical Novel: The Enlightenment and Scottish Literature* (Edinburgh, 1989)

Magan, William, *Umma-More: The Story of an Irish Family* (Salisbury, 1983)

Marcus, Phillip L., *Yeats and the Beginning of the Irish Renaissance* (Ithaca and London, 1970)

Masterson, Donald, and O'Shea, Edward, 'Code Breaking and Myth Making: The Ellis–Yeats Edition of Blake's Works' in Warwick Gould (ed.), *Yeats Annual No. 3* (London, 1985), pp. 53–80

Mattar, Sinéad Garrigan, *Primitivism, Science and the Irish Revival* (Oxford, 2004)

Maume, Patrick, 'Respectability against Ascendancy: The Banim Brothers and the Invention of the Irish Catholic Middle-Class Novel in the Age of O'Connell' in John Strachan and Alison O'Malley-Younger (eds.), *Ireland: Revolution and Evolution* (Bern, 2010), pp. 145–66

Melville, Joy, *Mother of Oscar: The Life of Jane Francesca Wilde* (London, 1994)

Mercier, Vivian, *The Irish Comic Tradition* (London, 1962)

Molony, John N., *A Soul Came into Ireland: Thomas Davis 1814–1845 – A Biography* (Dublin, 1996)

Moore, Daffyd R., 'The Critical Response to Ossian's Romantic Bequest' in Gerard Carruthers and Alan Rawes (eds.), *English Romanticism and the Celtic World* (Cambridge, 2003)

Moore, Jane, 'Thomas Moore as Irish Satirist' in David Duff and Catherine Jones (eds.), *Scotland, Ireland and the Romantic Aesthetic* (Lewisburg, Pa., 2007), pp. 152–71

Morash, Christopher, *Writing the Irish Famine* (Oxford, 1985)
—— *The Hungry Voice: The Poetry of the Irish Famine* (Dublin, 1989)
—— *A History of the Irish Theatre 1601–2000* (Cambridge, 2000)

Morrow John, 'Thomas Carlyle, "Young Ireland" and the "Condition of Ireland Question"', *Historical Journal*, 51, 3 (2008), pp. 643–67

Mulvey, Helen, *Thomas Davis and Ireland: A Biographical Study* (Washington, DC, 2003)

Murphy James H., *Catholic Fiction and Social Reality in Ireland 1873–1922* (Westport, Conn., 1997)

Murray, Damien, *Romanticism, Nationalism and Irish Antiquarian Societies 1840–1880* (Maynooth, 2000)

Murray, Paul, *From the Shadow of Dracula: A Life of Bram Stoker* (London, 2004)

Nicholson, Andrew, 'Byron and the "Ariosto of the North"' in Gerard Carruthers and Alan Rawes (eds.), *English Romanticism and the Celtic World* (Cambridge, 2003)

Nolan, Emer, 'Banim and the Historical Novel' in Jacqueline Belanger (ed.), *The Irish Novel in the Nineteenth Century: Facts and Fictions* (Dublin, 2005), pp. 80–93

—— *Catholic Emancipations: Irish Fiction from Thomas Moore to James Joyce* (Syracuse, NY, 2007)

Ó Cadhla, Stiofán, *Civilizing Ireland: Ordnance Survey 1824–1842 – Ethnography, Cartography, Translation* (Dublin, 2007)

Ó Ciosáin, Niall, *Print and Popular Culture in Ireland 1750–1850* (London, 1997)

O'Donoghue, Bernard, 'Poetry in Ireland' in Joe Cleary and Claire Connolly (eds.), *The Cambridge Companion to Modern Irish Culture* (Cambridge, 2005), pp. 173–89

O'Driscoll, Robert, *An Ascendancy of the Heart: Ferguson and the Beginnings of Modern Irish Literature in English* (Dublin, 1976)

Ó Gallchoir, Cliona, *Maria Edgeworth: Women, Enlightenment and Nation* (Dublin, 2007)

O'Halloran, Clare, 'Irish Re-creations of the Gaelic Past: The Challenge of Macpherson's *Ossian*', *Past and Present*, 124 (1989), pp. 69–85

—— *Golden Ages and Barbarous Nations: Antiquarian Debate and Cultural Politics in Ireland c. 1750–1800* (Cork, 2004)

—— 'Harping on the Past: Translating Antiquarian Learning into Popular Culture in Early Nineteenth-Century Ireland' in Melissa Calaresu, Filippo de Vivo and Joan Pau Rubies (eds.), *Exploring Cultural History: Essays in Honour of Peter Burke* (Farnham, Surrey, 2010), pp. 327–43

Patten, Eve, *Samuel Ferguson and the Culture of Nineteenth-Century Ireland* (Dublin, 2006)

Pittock, Murray, *Scottish and Irish Romanticism* (Oxford, 2008)

Portsmouth, Robert, *John Wilson Croker: Irish Ideas and the Creation of Modern Conservatism 1800–1835* (Dublin, 2010)

Pritchett, V. S., *The Living Novel* (London, 1946)

Reid, Colin, 'The Political and Cultural Life of Stephen Gwynn, with Particular Reference to the Period 1905–1926' (Ph.D., Queen's University, Belfast, 2008)

Robertson, Fiona, *Legitimate Histories: Scott, Gothic and the Authorities of Fiction* (Oxford, 1994)

Sage, Victor, *Horror Fiction in the Protestant Tradition* (London, 1988)

Sheehy, Jeanne, *The Rediscovery of Ireland's Past: The Celtic Revival 1800–1830* (London, 1980)

Showalter, Elaine, *Sexual Anarchy: Gender and Culture at the* Fin de Siècle (London, 1991)

Sloan, Barry, *The Pioneers of Anglo-Irish Fiction 1800–1850* (Totowa, NJ, 1987)

Spence, Joseph 'The Philosophy of Irish Toryism 1833–1852: A Study of Reactions to Liberal Reformism in Ireland in the Generation between the First Reform Act and the Famine, with Especial Reference to Expressions of National Feeling among the Protestant Ascendancy' (Ph.D., University of London, 1991)

—— 'Isaac Butt, Irish Nationality and the Conditional Defence of the Union 1833–1870' in D. George Boyce and Alan O'Day (eds.), *Defenders of the Union: A Survey of British and Irish Unionism since 1801* (London, 2001), pp. 65–89

Stafford, Fiona, *The Sublime Savage: A Study of James Macpherson and the Poems of Ossian* (Edinburgh, 1989)

Stewart, Bruce (ed.), *That Other World: The Supernatural and the Fantastic in Irish Literature and Its Contexts* (Gerrards Cross, 1998)

Thuente, Mary-Helen, *W. B. Yeats and Irish Folklore* (Dublin, 1980)

Toomey Deirdre, 'Who Fears to Speak of Ninety-Eight?' in Warwick Gould (ed.), *Yeats Annual No. 14: Yeats and the Nineties* (London, 2001)

Tracy, Robert, *The Unappeasable Host: Studies in Irish Identities* (Dublin, 1998)

Trevor-Roper, Hugh, *The Invention of Scotland: Myth and History* (London, 2008)

Trumpener Katie, *Bardic Nationalism: The Romantic Novel and the British Empire* (Princeton, 1997)

Valente, Joseph, *Dracula's Crypt: Bram Stoker, Irishness and the Question of Blood* (Chicago, 2002)

Wade, Allan, *A Bibliography of the Writings of W. B. Yeats* (London, 1958)

Webb, Timothy, ' "A Great Theatre of Outrage and Disorder": Figuring Ireland in the *Edinburgh Review* 1802–1829' in Duncan Wu and Massimiliano Demata (eds.), *British Romanticism and the* Edinburgh Review: *Bicentenary Essays* (London, 2003)

White, Harry, *Music and the Irish Literary Imagination* (Oxford, 2008)

Wilson A. N., *The Laird of Abbotsford: A View of Sir Walter Scott* (London, 1980)

Wilson, David A., *Thomas D'Arcy Magee. Vol. I: Passion, Reason and Politics 1825–1857* (Kingston, Ontario, 2008)

SOURCES FOR ILLUSTRATIONS

1. Manuscript draft of 'The Happy Shepherd' by W. B. Yeats, early 1880s, National Library of Ireland.
2. W. B. Yeats in 1886 by J. B. Yeats: frontispiece of *Mosada*, from National Library of Ireland copy.
3. Maria Edgeworth, engraving after a painting by Alonzo Chappell, Alamy/Interfoto.
4. Sydney Owenson [Lady Morgan] by Daniel Maclise, from *A Portrait Gallery of Illustrious Literary Characters, accompanied by notices chiefly by W. Maginn* (London, 1873), courtesy of Bodleian Libraries.
5. Title page of first edition of *The Wild Irish Girl*, courtesy of the National Library of Ireland.
6. Calton Hill, Edinburgh, by J. M. W. Turner, 1820. National Gallery of Scotland.
7. Christ's Cathedral, Dublin, by George Petrie, from T. K. Cromwell, *Excursions through Ireland* (1820–21).
8. Walter Scott kissing the Blarney Stone on his Irish tour in 1825, etching by Daniel Maclise in Rev. Francis Mahony, *The Reliques of Father Prout* (1836).

9. Tom Moore by Daniel Maclise, Victoria and Albert Museum/Forster Bequest.

10. John Banim. Getty Images.

11. Title page of first edition of *Captain Rock*, courtesy of the National Library of Ireland.

12. Title page of first edition of *Representative Irish Tales*, 1891, courtesy of the National Library of Ireland.

13. Jane Carlyle by Samuel Laurence, 1848, National Trust Picture Library/John Hammond.

14. Thomas Carlyle in 1845, Getty Images/Time and Life Pictures.

15. Charles Gavan Duffy by J. C. MacRae, after an unknown artist, National Portrait Gallery, London.

16. Thomas Davis's copy of the first issue of the *Nation*, courtesy of the Royal Irish Academy.

17. The Ordnance Survey conducting measurements at Lough Foyle, 1827, from W. Yolland, *An Account of the Measurement of the Lough Foyle Base* (1847), courtesy of the National Library of Ireland.

18. Thomas Davis by Frederick William Burton, National Gallery of Ireland.

19. Samuel Ferguson by Frederick Burton, 1848, National Gallery of Ireland.

20. Isaac Butt by John Butler Yeats, 1876, National Portrait Gallery, London.

21. Daniel Maclise, *The Marriage of the Princess Aoife of Leinster with Richard de Clare, Earl of Pembroke (Strongbow)*, 1854, National Gallery of Ireland.

SOURCES FOR ILLUSTRATIONS

22. Thomas Moore's *Irish Melodies*, first number, 1808, courtesy of the National Library of Ireland.
23. Dublin in 1829, Dublin City Public Libraries/Wilson.
24. John Mitchel, National Portrait Gallery, London.
25. Thomas Francis Meagher, from an engraving in *Harper's Weekly*, 1867, Topfoto/The Granger Collection, New York.
26. The Carlyles at home in Chelsea, 1858. National Trust Picture Library/John Hammond.
27. Carlyle, a photograph signed in Limerick, 24 July 1849, from Charles Gavan Duffy, *Conversations with Carlyle* (1892).
28. An Irish village towards the end of the Famine, 1849. Mary Evans Picture Library/*Illustrated London News* Ltd.
29. Lisselane, West Cork, home of the Bence-Jones family, under armed guard during the Land War, 1880, *Illustrated London News* Ltd.
30. Thomas Crofton Croker by Daniel Maclise, 1829, Victoria and Albert Museum/ Forster Bequest.
31. *A Fairy Dance* by Daniel Maclise, 1826, Victoria and Albert Museum.
32. Bram Stoker, 1884. Alamy/Lordprice Collection.
33. The restrained first edition of *Dracula*, courtesy of the British Library Board.
34. Sheridan Le Fanu, *c.* 1843, artist unknown (Private Collection).
35. Emmanuel Swedenborg by Per Krafft, 1766, Swedish National Portrait Gallery, Stockholm; Corbis/The Art Archive.

36. Samuel Forde, *The Fall of the Rebel Angels*, 1828. Crawford Gallery Cork.

37. William Wilde by J. H. Maguire, 1847, courtesy of the National Library of Ireland.

38. 'Speranza', Lady Wilde, by J. Morosoni (date unknown), National Gallery of Ireland.

39. William Carleton by John Slattery (date unknown), National Gallery of Ireland.

40. W. B. Yeats's 'The Curse of Cromwell', illustrated by Jack Yeats for the *Broadside* series printed by Cuala Press, 1937. © Estate of Jack B Yeats. All rights reserved, DACS 2011.

41. John O'Leary by J. B. Yeats, 1887. National Gallery of Ireland.

42. Early manuscript draft of *The Wanderings of Oisin* by W. B. Yeats, courtesy of the National Library of Ireland.

43. *King Goll* by J. B. Yeats, using W. B. Yeats as a model, engraving in *Leisure Hour* (September 1887), from an original now lost.

44. Max Beerbohm's cartoon of Yeats presenting George Moore to the Queen of the Fairies, 1904, the Bridgeman Art Library/Central Saint Martins College of Art and Design, London (original in Dublin City Gallery, The Hugh Lane).

45. Augusta Gregory, early 1900s, Getty/ George C. Beresford/ Hulton Archive.

46. *The Fairy Greyhound* by Jack Yeats, for *Irish Fairy Tales*, 1892.

47. A page of William Blake's *Marriage of Heaven and Hell*, annotated by W. B. Yeats in the early 1890s, courtesy of *Yeats Annual*.

48. W. B. Yeats by Althea Gyles, *c.* 1898, by permission of the Trustees of the British Museum. All rights reserved.
49. W. B. Yeats listening to Homer, as seen by Jack Yeats, *c.* 1887. Manuscript, Archives, and Rare Book Library, Emory University, GA.
50. A note by Yeats on talent and genius, 1887, courtesy of National Library of Ireland.

Despite my efforts, some copyright holders remained untraced at the time this book went to press. If you hold or administer rights for images published here, please contact the publisher. Any errors or omissions will be corrected in subsequent editions.

INDEX

Page numbers in *italics* indicate an illustration.

Withdrawn From Stock Dublin City Public Libraries

Withdrawn From Stock Dublin City Public Library